W9-CEN-132

BOOKS FROM ACADEMY LEADERSHIP PUBLISHING

The Accountability Compass: Moving from "The Blame Game" to Collaboration

The Core Values Compass: Moving from Cynicism to a Core Values Culture

The Corporate Compass: Providing Focus and Alignment to Stay the Course, 2nd Edition

My Father's Compass: Leadership Lessons for an Immigrant Son

The Leader's Compass: A Personal Leadership Philosophy Is Your Key to Success, 2nd Edition

Inspiring Leadership: Character and Ethics Matter

The ACCOUNTABILITY C🧭MPASS

Moving from "THE BLAME GAME" *to* COLLABORATION

Dennis F. Haley

Academy Leadership Publishing

ISBN: 978-0-9727323-9-0

Library of Congress Control Number: 2012910646

Academy Leadership books are available at special quantity
discounts to use as premiums and sales promotions, or for use
in corporate training programs. For more information, please
call Academy Leadership at 610-783-0630, or write to: 10120
Valley Forge Circle, King of Prussia, PA 19406.

Printed in the United States of America.

TABLE OF CONTENTS

PART ONE

CHAPTER 1

Boss or Bottleneck?

A cold winter rain tapped against the windows at Eaton/ Argosy Marketing as Guy Cedrick scrolled through the project management program on his laptop. Color-coded timelines for each of the firm's projects stretched across the screen. At the right margin, Guy typed in a series of reminders and new to-dos, adding to the list until it grew so long that he gave up trying to squeeze everything into a single day. With a resigned sigh, he pulled out his phone and texted a quick heads-up to his wife, Melanie: "Late night again. Sorry." Guy knew that Melanie wouldn't be happy about the fact that he'd be missing their family dinner—again—but he hoped she'd understand.

As if on cue, Linda Hutchinson appeared in Guy's doorway. "Are you finished with Julie's draft yet?" she asked. "We've had the design ready since yesterday." Linda, Eaton/Argosy's managing director, was referring to the first draft of promotional copy for Flavor Burst gum, a new client.

Immediately, Guy wished that Linda had come to ask him about one of the thousand other things on his to-do list, because he hadn't taken the time to look over the Flavor Burst copy. "I want to check this before we let it go," Guy said, hoping to stall. "This is the first thing we've ever sent these people. I want it to read right."

He looked at Linda for some understanding, but she offered him only a stone-faced stare.

"I needed to move this yesterday," she replied. Guy nodded as Linda walked toward his desk, knowing that she was right. Soon, though, her eyebrows rose and her expression softened as she peered over Guy's shoulder at the bright red to-do list running down the length of his computer screen. "Why don't you just send that copy right over to me and check it off that scary-looking list? You look pretty overloaded."

Guy couldn't argue with that assessment. He smiled and closed the lid on his laptop. "I think Ted has been sending us all his high-maintenance clients. What do you think?"

"What I think," Linda said, "as the traffic cop around here, is that a lot of the gridlock in this office is happening around your desk. The clients aren't getting difficult. You are."

Guy knew that Linda was trying to help, but he still felt the need to defend himself. "This is a new client," he reiterated. "I've got to make sure we set the right tone from the start. Then I can let go." He paused. "A little."

Linda glanced toward the rain-smeared window, then back at Guy. He recognized the rueful yet determined look on her face all too well, and braced himself for what she was about to say.

"I've seen a change in you since the sale," Linda told him. "Back before Argosy bought us, you were better at delegating. You had a much easier time leaving the creative work to your project managers when you had to worry about payroll, billing, back office, and receivables."

Two years earlier, the Eaton Group had been bought out by Argosy Marketing and Advertising, its larger crosstown rival in Philadelphia. Argosy's founder and owner, a formidable ad man named Ted Stone, chose to keep the Eaton Group employees together in a separate division called Eaton/Argosy that would specialize in new media. Guy, who had started out as a graphic designer with the Eaton Group and had eventually become its *de facto* chief operating officer, was promoted to creative director of the new division. Linda had been promoted from Eaton Group's head of multimedia production to Eaton/Argosy's managing director, the division's number-two position.

"Well, before the sale I didn't have Ted Stone's second guessing to worry about," Guy countered, reaching over to a stack of papers on the other side of his desk. He held up a partial printout of Julie's Flavor Burst text and caught Linda's eye. "Have *you* gone over this?"

"It's fine," Linda said, giving Guy the thumbs-up sign. "It's time to let the client see it."

Guy looked at the time. "I'm supposed to call Ted at 4:30," he said. "So I'll make you a deal. If I don't send you Julie's text in 20 minutes, move it along without me, okay?" Linda rolled her eyes and disappeared into the hallway.

The call with Ted was brief, but Ted's voice sounded cheery. "I want you to come by the office tomorrow at ten," he instructed Guy. "Something new has come up with MegaMart and CellMobile. There's someone I want you to meet."

Guy barely had a chance to confirm that he'd be at the meeting before Ted hung up the phone.

MegaMart and CellMobile were two of the firm's biggest clients. The previous year, Guy had led a successful nationwide product launch for the TrekPhone, an inexpensive device developed by CellMobile and sold by MegaMart. Both client companies were happy with the launch, but Ted hadn't given Guy's division any more work with either company since. Hoping that the mysterious person he was supposed to meet the next morning might lead to another high-profile project, Guy hopped out of his chair and went looking for Linda to tell her about Ted's call.

"I've been wondering if we'd ever hear from them again," Linda murmured with a look of surprise after Guy had updated her. "You know, they were tough to work with, but we've gotten a lot of mileage out of that launch. Think about it. How many new clients did we get on the strength of that one campaign?"

"At least a dozen," Guy estimated. "I hope they're launching an upgraded TrekPhone. There are so many things I'd like to try and do differently this time around."

The more Guy considered the possibility of going back to work with such high-profile clients, the more the day's little problems seemed to melt away. Glancing down, Guy suddenly remembered that he still was holding Julie's Flavor Burst promotional text in his hand. He handed it to Linda. "You can give this back to Julie. Let's send it. It's time to let the client see it."

Chapter 2

To Go Where No Cell Phone Has Gone Before

At first glance, Ted Stone's enormous corner office appeared to be vacant as Guy walked through its heavy double doors. The high-backed ergonomic leather chair behind Ted's oaken desk was empty. Only after he was several steps into the room did Guy spot Ted sitting on his office couch to the right. In a chair next to him was an unfamiliar man wearing a blue blazer and a floral bowtie. The man's small stature and delicate features reminded Guy of an elf, and despite the apprehension that Ted's office always evoked, he found himself suppressing a smile.

"Guy, say hello to Nigel Stamford," Ted instructed, motioning him over to their corner of the room. "He's a consultant visiting here from England."

Nigel gave a quick nod of his head and reached out to shake hands, the motion made awkward by his simultaneous attempt to stand. "Ted's told me many complimentary things about you," Nigel said as Guy's large hand swallowed his. "I'm very interested to hear more about that great campaign you did with MegaMart and CellMobile."

Obviously, Ted saw and correctly identified the confusion that registered on Guy's face. "Did you think we'd be meeting with someone from MegaMart or CellMobile?" he asked. It was as though he had read Guy's mind. "I'm sorry if I gave you that impression. This is a meeting *about* them, not with them."

Guy's heart sank. Ever since his conversation with Ted the previous evening, he'd thought of little else besides the prospect of relaunching the TrekPhone. He forced himself to bury his disappointment and pay attention to Ted as he took a seat.

"Nigel is an expert on mobile commerce and marketing," Ted began. "He's done some groundbreaking work in Britain, France, and Spain, where they've taken mobile commerce much further than anything we've done over here. Did you know that in parts of Europe you can use your cell phone as an actual substitute for your credit and debit cards?"

From the gleam in Ted's eyes, Guy surmised that his boss was very excited by this prospect. "They've got something called wave-and-pay, where shoppers pay for their items by simply waving their cell phones past a sensor at the checkout counter."

Guy had to admit that this wave-and-pay system sounded convenient. He made himself as comfortable as he could on the modern metal chair he'd chosen and settled in to find out what the point of this unusual meeting would be.

Taking the floor, Nigel explained how computer chips installed inside cell phones can perform the same function as the black strips of magnetic coding on the backs of credit and debit cards. These same chips can also pick up signals from wireless transmitters inside stores and allow retailers to send instant discounts and sales promotions directly to their shoppers' phones. When a shopper taps her phone against a display in the detergent aisle, Nigel explained, the system might automatically recognize her as a regular customer and send the phone an electronic coupon for an instantly reduced price on the detergent.

"People love shopping this way," Nigel assured Ted and Guy. "The surveys put consumer satisfaction rates at well over 80 percent. Shoppers love the discounts, and they *especially* appreciate not having to fumble in their wallets and handbags for coupons, cash, and credit cards." At this point, Nigel leaned forward and made eye contact with Ted, then Guy. "And the surveys reveal something else that's very important. Once people get accustomed to wave-and-pay shopping, they're hooked. They start avoiding retailers that don't offer it."

Nigel's speech had sold Guy on the perks of wave-and-pay, but despite his interest, he didn't see a clear angle for Argosy. "So, is MegaMart ready to do this?" he guessed, thinking out loud. "Do they want us to promote a rollout for this wave-and-pay system?"

"No, nothing like that," Ted responded. He shifted on the couch so that he faced Guy more directly. "This technology is not that new. We could have been using it in the U.S. years ago. But none of the big players over here have ever been able to get together on it. Now, though, thanks to our relationship with MegaMart and CellMobile, we might be a part of the solution."

Guy fiddled with one of his cuff links, the motion unconscious as he digested and dissected Ted's words. He thought he was beginning to understand where Ted was going with this. He was right.

"Both companies have agreed to work with Argosy on a special team, a working group that will identify one specific wave-and-pay system that all three companies can get behind," Ted continued, confirming Guy's suspicions. "With MegaMart as the dominant retailer in the U.S. and CellMobile as the dominant wireless company, the two could set a new national standard for wave-and-pay if only—" Ted's eyes widened in shock as he was interrupted mid-sentence by Nigel.

"Greg, both companies *need* us to help them with this," he said in a rush, unaware that he had gotten Guy's name wrong *and* managed to cut off a man who wasn't used to being interrupted. "MegaMart can't afford to go ahead and install a wave-and-pay system in its U.S. stores because none of the cell phone companies here are making compatible phones. And CellMobile doesn't want to begin making phones that are capable of wave-and-pay until they see retailers start investing in compatible systems. So it's a chicken-and-egg problem. Which comes first?" Nigel paused to take a breath for the first time in his speech.

"That's why I approached Ted with this idea of working with CellMobile and MegaMart," he continued, spreading his hands as though presenting a gift. "If we can bring together the biggest retailer and the biggest mobile company and get them to agree to a joint launch of a single wave-and-pay system, we can work on all the cross-promotional efforts that will help make it a success."

Guy nodded, buying himself a few moments to put together a tactful response. "Let me see if I understand what you're saying. MegaMart and CellMobile won't be our clients?"

"No," said Ted, overriding Nigel, who had just opened his mouth to respond. "We're *partners* with them. Wave-and-pay is going to need a lot of creative promotion and marketing, or people won't give it a try. That would be our contribution in this partnership. We'll make sure that the system MegaMart and CellMobile agree upon will have the technical capacity to support all the in-store specials and electronic coupons that we'll need to make the launch successful. "

Nigel nodded his head vigorously the entire time Ted was speaking, obviously not offended in the slightest at having been temporarily thrust out of the spotlight. He picked up where Ted had left off. "We'll need to identify a wave-and-pay system that will work seamlessly with promotional software to deliver features like the detergent discount I was telling you about. Without those kinds of promotions, the surveys show that people won't switch. They'll stick to the familiar. They'll keep using cash and cards."

This time, it was Ted who had been nodding while Nigel spoke—but he never took his eyes off of Guy. *For better or for worse*, Guy thought, *they're about to drop the bomb on me.*

"U.S. retail is a $6 trillion industry," Ted said. "And with this working group, Guy, you will help revolutionize it."

"Me?" Blindsided, Guy couldn't think of anything else to say. Forget being articulate; it was a struggle to simply wrap his brain around what Ted had just told him.

"Yes," Ted confirmed, flashing what Guy assumed was supposed to be a congratulatory smile. "I want you to lead this working group, get this thing kick-started. Nigel will be part of your team from Argosy. So will Mike Andrews from product marketing here, as well as a few of our mobile commerce specialists."

Guy scrubbed a hand through his short hair, still dumbfounded. All he could think about was his long to-do list back at the office. Now add this. *Might as well bring a sleeping bag to work with me. I'm never gonna make it home in time for dinner ever again!* he thought. *Melanie's* really *not going to be happy about this.*

"I know this is sudden," Ted conceded, breaking into Guy's gloomy thoughts. "And I know that we've never discussed doing a project remotely resembling anything like this before. But things are changing fast in this industry. We need to seize opportunities when they come along."

"How sudden are we talking about?" Guy asked.

"We want a report in ten weeks," Ted told him. "If your group can recommend one system that all three companies can sign off on, then we'll get the lawyers together, set up a jointly owned subsidiary, and get to work. But this first part is critical." He pointed his index finger at Guy for emphasis. "In ten weeks or less, we want your working group to sort through all the different wave-and-pay systems and vendors already out there and find which one or which combination is the most promising."

No pressure, Guy added mentally.

"Think about that $6 trillion, Guy," Nigel urged, a look that Guy could describe only as "dreamy" taking over his face. "If this works out, Argosy will have a little piece of that cash flow, a little transaction charge on every wave-and-pay sale. One percent of $6 trillion is $60 billion. A *thousandth* of one percent is $60 million! Even the tiniest slice of annual retail spending is still an enormous sum of money." By this point, Nigel's voice was downright reverent.

Still not sure exactly how to respond, Guy raised his eyebrows and offered a silent nod, hoping he didn't look too much like the proverbial "deer in the headlights."

"Look, it's a lot to take in, I know," Ted admitted. "Nigel has put together a three-ring binder here for you. Take it home this evening, look up some of the materials online, and see if you can get a feel for how this thing might go. Nigel needs to fly back to London tomorrow afternoon, so why don't you stop by and meet us after lunch. I'll call you later to tell you where we'll be."

With that, Ted stood up to signal that the meeting was over. "I've got another appointment downstairs in a few minutes," he explained as he ushered Nigel and Guy to the elevators. "I'll see you gentlemen tomorrow!"

Nigel and Guy shared a silent ride to the lobby until Guy caught Nigel looking up at him with a crooked smile just before the doors opened. "Exciting, isn't it?" Nigel asked.

"Very exciting," Guy replied by rote. But most of what he felt inside was dread.

Chapter 3

The Binder Blues

Back in his office, Guy cracked open Nigel's binder, a bit apprehensive about what he might find. As he scanned the pages filled with technical data, his mental functions started fogging over the way they always did in high school calculus class. Every line of text contained another mysterious technical term. Near-field communications. Location-aware applications. GSM triangulation. It was almost like trying to decipher a foreign language. If it weren't for the illustrations of smiling people pushing shopping carts, Guy might have mistaken the binder for a NASA flight manual.

Looking up from the mind-boggling binder, Guy noticed Freddie Jencks strolling past his door. Freddie was a junior staffer who had been hired recently in product marketing, and Guy knew that he had spent the previous summer traveling through Europe. *Maybe he can help me*, Guy thought as he jumped up and stuck his head into the hallway to hail Freddie.

"From your time in Europe, Freddie, do you know anything about this pay-by-cell-phone system?" Guy asked once Freddie was seated across from his desk.

"Yeah, it's actually pretty cool," Freddie said, a grin spreading across his freckled face. "In one city, I forget which one, I saw people waving their phones all over the place. Parking meters. Vending machines. I even saw an old lady use it in a grocery store. She must have been, like, 50 years old." Guy suppressed a smile at Freddie's idea of "old." Another 15 years, and he'd be there himself.

"So can you tell me anything about how the actual transaction works?" Guy asked. "Did the customers have to change the settings on their phones or punch in a code number at the checkout counter?"

Freddie shrugged. "Sorry, I didn't notice," he said. "I only remember how funny-looking it was to see people waving their phones around. I couldn't do it myself because I had my American phone with me. It wasn't good for anything over there—except making super-expensive phone calls."

"Yeah, I bet," Guy commiserated. "Hey, thanks for your help! I might ask to pick your brain again in the next few weeks."

As Freddie left his office, Guy looked at the clock. It was 3 p.m. If he left for home now, he'd get three hours of peace and quiet to look over all this material before his wife, Melanie, came home with their two little girls. If he stayed in the office, though, who knew how many interruptions he'd get? That thought was all it took to make Guy decide to pack up his briefcase and head for the door with the hulking binder under his arm.

He had made it through Eaton/Argosy's central grouping of workstations and had just pressed the "down" button on the elevator when Linda Hutchinson called his name. Jogging up, she asked, "Hey, what's the news with TrekPhone?"

Guy was at a loss to explain what had transpired without resorting to an hour-long explanation. "Not happening," he said, cutting to the chase as the elevator door opened to the sound of a chime. He held up Nigel's black binder. "I'll tell you about this thing in the morning." Guy's last sight as the elevator door closed was Linda shaking her head and throwing her hands up in mock defeat.

When Guy arrived home, the house was cool, dark, and blessedly quiet. Guy knew he couldn't ask for conditions better suited to concentration, so he unlocked the binder's ring clips and started to spread all the material across the dining room table. When he reached the center of the table, his progress was impeded by an antique vase filled with flowers. Guy smiled, guessing that this was one of Melanie's newest purchases that he'd just never noticed before. He picked up the vase as gently as he could and moved it to a side table.

Soon, Guy had come to the discouraging realization that the pages of technical data in front of him were so confusing they defied organization. First, he tried sifting out all of the documents pertaining to pilot projects and experimental systems. He put them aside in one pile. Then he took the rest of the documents, which described currently working systems. These all went into another, larger pile.

Next, Guy decided to try breaking down this big pile into geographic regions. But some companies did business in both Europe and Asia, and there was too much overlap. So he tried dividing the pile according to system specifications, until he realized he didn't understand the terminology well enough. Finally, he admitted to himself he had no way of making sense of the material. How could there be so many proprietary approaches and so many incompatible protocols for the same simple task? If there was a good reason, Guy couldn't see it.

"You've really outdone yourself this time, Ted!" he muttered under his breath, hoping he'd be able to present some sort of coherent response to his boss and Nigel the next day.

At 6:35, Melanie and the girls burst through the door. Nine-year-old Donna leapt into Guy's arms and proudly displayed a plastic bag full of hamster food. "We're putting Lumpy and Betsy on a new diet!" she exclaimed. Then she and her four-year-old sister, Molly, ran down the hallway toward the hamster cage.

Melanie set a bag of groceries on the kitchen counter. "What's all this?" she asked, nodding toward the dining room table and raising one eyebrow.

"It's the latest surprise from Ted Stone," Guy told her. He began to explain how the wave-and-pay system worked and how Argosy might fit in to the picture, but trailed off when he noticed the distracted look on Melanie's face.

"Hey, where's the new vase?" she asked.

Guy pointed to the side table. "Didn't want to break it while I was playing my fun game of 'rearrange-Nigel's-binder.' Did you buy that today?"

"Yup," she said, sounding pleased. "It's one of my better finds." Melanie had begun spending her mornings dealing in antiques. It was a skill she had learned from her parents, who ran a small shop in the seaside town where she was raised.

"This vase reminded me of a 19th-century piece we had in the shop when I was growing up," she elaborated, walking over to the side table and bending down to inspect the vase more closely. "I think my father overpriced it because he liked having it around. That drove my mother crazy."

"Was it expensive?" Guy asked. He was beginning to worry whether Melanie's new hobby was going to put a drag on the household's finances. Melanie had left a career in accounting when their first daughter was born, but now that their youngest daughter was in preschool, she had talked about returning to work.

"I paid two hundred," Melanie responded, straightening up. "But I'll get more than that for it when I'm ready to sell. For now I like looking at it on the dining room table—that is, whenever you're done with the table." She scanned the printed materials Guy had spread out before him. "So what's all this about?"

"This," Guy said, making a sweeping gesture that took in the entire paper-strewn table, "is what Ted thinks is the next big revolution in retail shopping." He decided to make Melanie a consumer test subject. "Here's a question for you. Instead of paying for groceries with our debit card, how would you like to pay by using your cell phone?"

Melanie frowned. "How would I pay with a phone? That doesn't make any sense."

"They're already doing it in Europe and Asia," Guy told her. "Instead of swiping a card or paying cash, you wave your phone over a little sensor pad right at the checkout counter. It's called wave-and-pay."

"I guess I could do that," she said, taking a seat next to him. "It sounds a little more convenient than fishing for cards or cash in my bag. Who's the client?"

"It's a new project we're doing with MegaMart and CellMobile."

"And that's all there is to it?" she asked. "Just wave and pay with your phone."

"No, there's more," Guy explained. "Picture yourself walking down the shopping aisle and your phone starts receiving electronic coupons. The store has a wireless system that picks up your phone signal, registers you as a repeat customer, and sends your phone coupons and special price discounts based on your shopping history. Then your savings are added up and deducted from your bill at the checkout, when you make the wave-and-pay move with your phone."

"If it gets rid of all those little paper coupons, then that sounds pretty great," Melanie said. "I wouldn't miss paper coupons at all. Either I forget to bring them with me or I forget to use them when I'm at the store."

"Okay then," Guy responded. He leaned back in his chair to stretch some of the kinks out of his back. "That's why Ted says this is going to revolutionize retail. Judging from what you've told me, he's probably right."

Melanie glanced at the pictures on the materials spread out over the table. "But wait a minute," she cautioned. "What if I lose my phone like I did last fall? Would anyone be able to take my phone and go on a waving and spending binge?"

Guy hadn't thought of that potential issue yet. "Good question, Honey. I don't know the answer. But I'll make sure to find out."

Melanie thought for a few more moments. "You've got to promote this for MegaMart?"

"Well, not really—at least, not yet," Guy qualified, thumbing through the stack of papers nearest to him. "Ted wants me to work with MegaMart and CellMobile on a special group to analyze these systems. He wants me to *lead* the group. The trouble is, I don't understand the technology at all. So I came home early to try and figure it all out. I don't know how I can lead on something I don't understand."

"Well, this looks like a job for an electrical engineer or a systems analyst," Melanie mused. "Why would Ted want you to be the leader?"

"He likes how I worked with MegaMart and CellMobile on the TrekPhone project a couple of years back," Guy explained.

"Besides, engineers and analysts have a tin ear for consumer habits. They'd be liable to recommend a system that only engineers and analysts would love. Still, most of what I'm looking at here is incomprehensible to me. I get the general idea, but the technical information may as well be written in Greek."

Melanie scooted her chair closer to Guy and looked over at the papers in his hands. She gave a low whistle and shook her head. "This writing is worse than the tax code! What does this mean?" She pointed at one line and read aloud: "Near-field communications can offer compatible interface with existing POS contactless readers that are compliant with ISO 14443."

"POS is point-of-sale," Guy translated, relieved that he could answer at least one part of her question. "It's the checkout counter, in layman's terms. But the rest of that text is a complete mystery to me."

The two sat in silence. Melanie unfolded a systems diagram that looked as complex as a government organizational chart. "Do you understand any of this one?" she asked as she looked it over.

"Nope. I don't even know what it's supposed to show." Guy pinched the bridge of his nose between his thumb and forefinger and sighed.

Off in the next room, the hamster cage was rattling as Molly and Donna fed Lumpy and Betsy their fresh straw. Melanie kept flipping through the materials. "Ted can't possibly expect you to digest all this material in a few weeks," she said. "He must have some reason for thinking you can run this project without understanding these details."

"Ted doesn't know the details himself," Guy replied. "That's what's got me worried. He wants me to take this on without having any idea how complicated it is. I've been feeling sick, sicker every hour, and I've had it since only 11 this morning. "

Melanie put her arm around Guy's shoulders and pulled him close enough to kiss his cheek. "Maybe you should talk to Stanley again," she offered. "He's always had a good read on what Ted is thinking."

Stanley Sabato, their next door neighbor, was a retired Navy Captain who had given Guy some valuable leadership advice during the merger with Argosy. Melanie was right about Stanley's ability to read Ted Stone. But Guy suspected that this latest problem might be too far outside Stanley's experience.

"I'm not sure I could even *describe* this project to Stanley," Guy muttered. He felt defeated. "It's a high-tech problem, and, if you hadn't noticed, Stanley still has a rotary-dial phone in his kitchen."

Melanie chuckled and squeezed Guy's shoulder. She couldn't argue with his assessment of Stanley's technological savvy, or lack thereof.

Guy stared at a page of technical specifications. "It would take me months to learn what all this means. Ted says he needs this project to start in two weeks, and I've already got too much on my plate."

"Well, on a slightly different note, it's nice to see you home before 7:00," Melanie commented. On most evenings, Guy didn't return from work until after 8:00, when the children were already asleep. "Do you think Ted would excuse you from this project if you explained that you're just too busy?"

Guy shook his head. "'Too busy' is never a good excuse with Ted. And the funny thing is, I really *want* to be a part of this group. Since this morning I've had about a dozen good ideas on how to run the wave-and-pay product launch. But how can I lead the group? Producing a report in ten weeks? I'm not prepared for it."

"When do you need to give Ted an answer?"

"I'm meeting with him again tomorrow afternoon. I have to figure out what to say between now and then."

Melanie rose and put her arms around her husband. "Good luck with that," she said, kissing him on the back of his neck. "I'm going to get the girls ready for bed. Please put the vase back on the table when you're done."

Guy reassembled the contents of Nigel's binder as best he could. His effort to organize the materials had left everything out of order. Amid the clicking and snapping of the binder clips, Guy could be heard muttering under his breath, rehearsing his lines for the next day's meeting with Ted.

CHAPTER 4

At Sea

The next afternoon, Guy was scheduled to meet Ted and Nigel at a downtown restaurant at 1:30. The two men had finished eating their lunches when Guy approached their table, Nigel's three-ring binder under his arm. Guy took a seat and laid the binder as well as a separate stack of printouts on an empty chair next to him.

"So what do you think?" Ted asked, clapping his hands together. "Pretty exciting, huh?"

Nigel looked at Guy, flashing his crooked smile. "Yeah, what do you think?"

"It's exciting," Guy agreed. "It's very exciting. I've started a list of ideas about how to get shoppers to switch to wave-and-pay. The possibilities for target marketing are endless. If MegaMart is willing to go deep enough with the discounts and the loyalty points, then I see what you both were talking about yesterday. It's a retail revolution."

Clearly, Nigel liked Guy's assessment of wave-and pay, since his crooked smile got even wider. "And you know what's next?"

he asked Guy. "Drivers' licenses and passports. It's already in the works in a few countries. The mobile phone is going to replace the billfold in your back pocket."

Nigel's face took on a dreamy look again as he continued to imagine a wallet-free future. "In five years, your daughters will ask you, 'Daddy, what's a wallet?'"

"So what about the working group, Guy?" Ted asked, interrupting Nigel's daydream and bringing them all back to reality. "Where's your list of ideas on how you're going to run that?"

Here we go, Guy thought, hoping that he could navigate the conversation without causing Ted to question his abilities. Before presenting his reaction to the binder, he motioned toward a passing waiter and asked for a glass of water. He was probably going to need it.

"Well, those technical materials did leave me wondering whether I'm the best person to take the lead," Guy said. He strained to sound positive. "I feel like I would be way in over my head. I'm ready to contribute right away on the promotions and marketing parts, but I've got some serious concerns about being the group leader."

Nigel jumped in. "Don't worry about all the technical details. I'll be there to help with that. And you'll soon find it's not as awfully complicated as it seems."

Ted held up his hand to stop Nigel. "We should let Guy finish what he wants to say, Nigel. Let's hear him out. What's your concern, Guy?"

Nigel stared across the table, almost without blinking, as Guy began again. "I understand the retail part pretty well," he confirmed. "But if we need to settle on one system in a short time frame, there are all these choices to be made involving hardware, software, engineering, electronics. There must be a dozen different wireless wavelength standards for wave-and-pay, and each standard has a half-dozen optional transmission ranges and power requirements for compatible phones..."

"No, no, no, no," Nigel blurted out, waving his hand as though trying to waft away Guy's doubts. "It's not as bad as all that. There are only two alternate wireless frequencies worth talking about in the U.S. and maybe six different transmission protocols we need to assess and choose from."

Guy tried to turn Nigel's interruption to his advantage. "You see? I didn't know that. There's a lot I don't know. As much as I want to be a part of this group, I think the group would work best if it were run by someone with a working knowledge of the technology."

As usual, Ted was blunt. "You still haven't said what your concern is."

At that moment, the waiter returned with Guy's water. "Thanks," he said, grateful for the momentary interruption because it allowed him a few seconds to formulate his answer. He turned his attention back to the two men at the table.

"My concern is that as leader, I'd end up wasting a lot of time, money, and good will with two very important clients," Guy explained as he squeezed the lemon slice on the glass's rim into the water. "I'd be afraid I might lead us into some flawed or second-rate technology because I'm too ignorant to make good decisions. Or, we might miss the deadlines because I don't know enough to get us past the stumbling blocks along the way."

Nigel jumped in again. "I think you should also keep in mind that we're under no pressure to find the absolute perfect solution. We only need to get a passable system in the works and get it done fast."

"Nigel's right about that, Guy," Ted confirmed, nodding in the other man's direction. "That's the advantage we enjoy by working with MegaMart and CellMobile on our side. These two companies are so big that any system they settle on, even a slightly flawed one, will likely become the U.S. standard."

"It happens all the time," Nigel added. "Whenever there's a fight over competing technologies, the winner is almost always decided by market power, not technical excellence."

"No one's got more market power than MegaMart," Ted explained, looking satisfied. "If we can get MegaMart and CellMobile to commit to one wave-and-pay standard, all the other retailers and phone makers will need to license that standard to use it for themselves. And Argosy will get a little cut of all those licensing fees."

Guy sipped his water, digesting what he had just heard. Ted's words made sense, but Guy still wasn't sure he should—or could—take the lead on the project.

"It's like the railroads," Nigel said in a lecturing tone. He fingered the corner of his bowtie—today it was decorated with tiny polka dots—as he spoke. "The first railroads in the 1800s had to make their tracks compatible with coal cart tracks, which were really narrow so they could fit down in the mine tunnels. Now almost every railroad in the world uses the same skinny 1.4-meter track gauge, merely because that was the size of coal cart tracks in England in 1814. It's crazy when you think about it…"

"That's very interesting, Nigel," Ted interjected. "But I'm not sure it addresses Guy's concern."

"Well, it does, a little," Guy offered. He nodded toward Nigel, who looked a bit disappointed at having his railroad lesson interrupted. "I hear what you're saying, that we don't have to try to be perfect. Even if we arrive at a wave-and-pay system with some flaws, its chief advantage would be that it came first, and with strong backing."

"Exactly." Nigel's expression regained its elfish exuberance upon learning that he and Guy were on the same page. "There's only one reason why no U.S. retailer has ever made a move on wave-and-pay. Every one of them is waiting to follow MegaMart. And now MegaMart and CellMobile are ready to follow us—if we're ready to lead."

"If *you're* ready to lead, Guy," Ted qualified, catching Guy's eye.

Guy took another sip of his water, then picked up the binder and started flipping through the pages in an attempt to hide his nerves. He could feel himself being talked into something he did not want to do.

"Ted, I look at these reports and they read like a foreign language to me," he said, deciding that honesty was the best policy—even if his concerns frustrated his boss. "What if I get into a meeting with MegaMart and CellMobile and get eaten alive? I can't believe there's no one on the tech side at Argosy who's better prepared for this than I am."

"Maybe there is someone," Ted conceded.

Guy felt some of the tension constricting his chest loosen for a moment—until Ted fixed him with another stare.

"But more importantly than understanding the tech stuff, you've worked with MegaMart and CellMobile before, Guy. You know how they work together. You also know how they don't always work together so well. You've led one big, successful project with them, and now all I'm asking is that you do it again."

Yeah, all *he's asking is for me to add about a million more glass balls to the ones I'm already juggling—and not to let any of them drop,* Guy thought, staring into his water as though the solutions to all of his concerns were hidden in its depths.

Nigel stood up, interrupting Guy's morose reverie. "Excuse me, gentlemen, but I'm going to have to get going in a few minutes," he said, laying his cloth napkin on the table. Then he headed off toward the men's room.

Once Nigel was out of sight, Ted leaned forward and lowered his voice. "No one understands all of this, Guy. Not really. The retailers, the cell phone companies, the equipment manufacturers, they're all scared to take the risk of being wrong. It's a standoff. They're all waiting for someone else to go first. We need to seize the day, before someone else does."

Then Ted said something that made an enormous impression on Guy. "There are plenty of times when a problem needs a solution and no one has the whole answer. Instead, lots of people have pieces of the answer. So they all stumble around, maybe for years, looking for some special person who can give them the whole answer. And they never find that person because usually that person doesn't exist."

Ted paused and let that thought settle in. Guy gazed at the swirl of pedestrians walking by the restaurant's plate-glass front window and wondered how many of them were also poised to potentially accomplish something great...if only they stopped looking for someone with the whole answer and started collaborating.

"What they need to do," Ted continued, echoing Guy's thoughts, "is find a leader to help them assemble all the pieces of the solution, because it's all there, right in their hands. And that leader might be someone who holds none of the pieces. It might be someone completely ignorant of the technical details required to arrive at the solution."

"Someone like me," Guy said. He knew now where Ted was headed.

"Yes, someone like you," Ted confirmed. "I don't think you need to know that many details in order to keep everyone together and moving forward. You can persuade them to cooperate and help them hash out their differences. You can make sure all the pieces come together, even if you don't know every last thing about those pieces."

Then Ted leaned toward Guy the way he did whenever he wanted Guy to know he was serious. "That's what I need from you now."

"I appreciate that, Ted," Guy said with mixed feelings. He was glad that Ted obviously had so much faith in his abilities, but he was still worried that he was getting in over his head. He picked up an inch-thick pile of printouts. "So what should I do? I'm supposed to be the leader, but I look at these documents and I don't know where to start. I feel completely at sea."

"At sea?" Ted smiled. "Well, if you're at sea, then you're lucky, because you've got that sea captain right next door to help you out!"

Ted was still laughing at his little joke when Nigel rejoined them. He told Nigel about Guy's neighbor Stanley, the retired Navy Captain.

Ted turned to Guy as they rose from the table. "I'm serious. Go see Stanley and see what he thinks. If Stanley tells you that you're absolutely wrong for this job, that you're not cut out for it, I'll trust his judgment."

There was nothing else Guy could say. They walked Nigel to the corner, where he caught a cab back to his hotel. Then the two men walked the three blocks back to Argosy's office tower.

Ted spoke first. "I have to say, Guy, I was a little embarrassed by the way you put up such a fight in front of Nigel."

Guy felt the tips of his ears warm up, even though he really didn't believe he had anything to be ashamed of. "I don't like feeling so unprepared at the start of a project," he explained. "The stakes are so high. I would think you'd want someone like Nigel running this group."

"Really?" Ted looked at Guy as though he couldn't believe what he heard. "Why is that?"

"He's got the smarts and the experience," Guy responded, pushing the button to activate the crosswalk signal as they waited at an intersection. "The other members of this group will listen to him because he's been doing wave-and-pay for years in Europe. He'll know how to organize our work to minimize risk and error. He'll know where problems are most likely to crop up. I won't know how to do any of that."

"I don't hear you calling Nigel a leader, though," Ted said as they and a few other pedestrians walked across the street. "Did you see how he forgot your name five minutes after meeting you? How he interrupts to go on and on about railroad tracks? How he races off to the men's room when I'm practically in mid-sentence? And how many times did he tell you that you were mistaken or flat-out wrong?"

Guy nodded in acknowledgment of Ted's point. "I lost count."

"I lost count, too," Ted agreed. "But MegaMart and CellMobile *won't* lose count. How long do you think they'll stay at the table if he's sitting at the head of it, lecturing them, interrupting them, telling them how they're wrong about this, that, and the other thing?"

"I see your point," Guy said. And he did. Like it or not, Nigel's technical knowledge alone wasn't enough to qualify him to lead this project.

"I haven't even gotten to my point." Ted stopped walking for a moment, oblivious to the fact that he had just turned himself and Guy into a mid-sidewalk obstacle for other office workers who were returning from lunch.

"The real point to all of this, Guy, is that I see huge long-term problems for our company. Profit margins are getting thinner every quarter because clients keep negotiating our fees downward and there's nothing we can do to stop them, short of telling them to leave. About six months ago, it dawned on me that if we don't make some changes soon, we're liable to ride this company right into the ground."

That prognosis came as a shock to Guy, but he understood immediately that Ted was right. "So that's why we're partnering on this instead of billing by the hour?"

"We've got to stretch," Ted confirmed. "This is one of four or five attempts we're making to reinvent ourselves, so we're not just another run-of-the-mill advertising and marketing shop."

The two men started walking again as Ted continued talking. "The other day I caught a glimpse on television of that old Woody Allen movie *Sleeper*. He plays this crazy guy who gets cryogenically frozen in 1973 and then they thaw him out in 2173. When he finds out he's been asleep for 200 years, his first reaction is, 'I bought Polaroid at seven. It must be up millions by now!'"

"Polaroid?" Guy asked. "Is that company even around any more?"

"Exactly," said Ted. "Back in 1973, when they made that movie, Polaroid had the market cornered on instant film photography. It probably seemed like this invincible high-tech company that would be around forever. But in the 1990s, when digital cameras came along, Polaroid refused to change until it was way too late. The company went belly up in 2001. It took less than seven years for Polaroid to go from market leader to liquidation."

The two men arrived in front of Argosy's building as Ted continued his thought. "That could be us. In five years, we might become another Polaroid. Maybe less than five years."

Guy listened in shocked silence. He'd never heard Ted, a confident and universally respected ad man, talk this way before.

"It's useless to resist new technologies," Ted said. "I accepted that much a long time ago. But now I've decided it's too dangerous to wait around and see which new technology wins out. We need to take chances and stake our claim to what we think might be the winner. That's wave-and-pay, Guy. It's the next big thing in retailing and mobile commerce, and we can be a part of it while all our competitors are standing on the sidelines."

Guy's mind reeled at the possibilities. "That's very smart," was the only thing he could think to say.

"It all begins by getting Nigel and MegaMart and CellMobile and a bunch of other smart people to all start singing from the same song sheet," Ted asserted, ticking off each of the groups on his fingers. "We have one opportunity to get out ahead of the pack here. If we don't use this advantage right away, we could lose it forever."

With that, Ted looked at his watch and clapped Guy on the shoulder. "Guy, you're a lot younger than me. You're the one who should be worried most about the future of this industry. There are fundamental changes happening fast in every industry. As far as I can see, the future belongs to people willing to change with the times and tolerate a little uncertainty along the way. That means sometimes you take the lead before you know all the answers. Or any of the answers, for that matter."

Ted softened his words with a smile. "So go talk to Stanley about this. I know that he went through some big changes in his Naval career. Ask him what he would do."

Before Ted disappeared through the revolving doors of Argosy's building, Guy had already reached for his phone and was scrolling through his contacts list. He hoped Stanley could see him that evening.

CHAPTER 5

Fear Factor

There was an antique Chippendale writing desk in the middle of the living room floor when Guy got home that evening. Melanie was adjusting the protective bubble wrap taped around its legs.

"Another big find?" Guy asked, bending down to give her a kiss.

"The real find is that I've already got a buyer lined up," Melanie replied. "I found an interior decorator ready to give me $3,500." She grinned up at him. "And guess how much I paid for it?"

"I don't know. Three thousand dollars?" Guy would be the first to admit that he knew next to nothing about the value of antiques.

"Noooo," she laughed. "It wouldn't be worth my trouble if I paid $3,000." She put her hand on the desktop and announced, "I bought it for $2,100."

Guy was speechless and genuinely impressed. "You made $1,400 on one desk in one day?"

His wife nodded her head with pride.

"Wow, I think I might be in the wrong business," Guy joked as he took off his suit coat and laid it over the back of a chair.

"I don't know about that," Melanie told him. "But I'm beginning to think I was in the wrong business with accounting. This is more flexible and it's a lot more fun. I love the game of it. The bargain hunting. Trying to figure out how low I can get the seller to go."

"Seriously, Honey, sounds like you did a great job today. And you've got a definite talent for reading people," Guy said as they walked toward the kitchen together. "You know how yesterday you suggested I go talk to Stanley about that wave-and-pay project? Well, that's exactly what Ted asked me to do today."

Melanie's smile fell from her face. "So Ted's not letting you out of leading that group?" she asked. "This means you're probably not going to make it home until 9:00 each night. You know how sad the girls get when they don't get to see you before bed. Not to mention the fact that your wife likes to have you around, too!"

"I know how you feel," Guy replied, and he meant it. "But Ted says he needs me. He told me to go to Stanley for advice, and that if Stanley says I'm wrong for the project, he'll accept Stanley's verdict." Guy paused. "But I think he was kidding."

Nevertheless, Guy took the short walk across his lawn and up the steps leading to Stanley Sabato's house after he had eaten dinner. Stanley answered the door and immediately invited Guy inside to his study. As he had in the past, Stanley listened patiently as Guy described his predicament.

"If I hear you correctly," Stanley said after Guy had finished, "you think Ted's making a mistake. He's putting you in a role where you're bound to fail. He's sure you're the right guy for the job, and you're sure you're the wrong guy."

Guy nodded, since that neatly summed up the whole situation. "Exactly. I told Ted that if he puts me in a room with a bunch of tech folks from CellMobile and MegaMart, it will take them about five minutes to see through me. They'll go back and tell their supervisors that this project is going nowhere, that it's a waste of time."

Stanley raised his eyebrows, deepening the faint wrinkles that were etched across his forehead. "That's the only outcome you see?"

"I can see muddling through a few meetings," Guy conceded with a shrug. "But when we get bogged down and behind schedule, when it's clear I'm clueless about how to get us back on track, then I can see Ted calling me up to say that MegaMart and CellMobile have quit the project." He sighed. "It might go that way."

"But you'd have help, wouldn't you?" Stanley looked puzzled. "What about that British fellow? He'd be there to advise on the technical details, right?"

"Nigel knows a lot," Guy admitted. "He'll have a lot of credibility with the others because he's worked on wave-and-pay in Europe. That's why I told Ted that I thought Nigel should lead the group. I should be there only to discuss my area of expertise, the Argosy perspective on promoting wave-and-pay."

A small smile tugged at the corner of Stanley's mouth. "But Ted doesn't want Nigel to lead, does he?"

"No. He doesn't think Nigel is a leader." Once again, Guy was impressed by the depth of the former submarine Captain's insight.

Stanley's smile widened. He was clearly pleased to have been correct. Then he leaned forward toward Guy. "Do *you* think Nigel is a leader?"

"No," Guy admitted. "I don't think he is, either. But he's bright and knowledgeable, so he might be able to get by. What I really think is that Ted is panicking. He's talked to me about how the industry is changing and how Argosy's got to change with it. But I'm not sure even he knows what he's doing. I think he might be throwing me into this role because he's got no one else."

Stanley heaved a sigh. "My cell phone is five years old," he admitted. "I have trouble saving phone numbers on it, so I don't think I'll ever use it to pay for groceries. And, frankly, I think it would be weird to have my phone feeding me coupons while I'm shopping. As you can see, I prefer paper *everything*." Stanley gestured toward the back corner of his study, which housed several solid filing cabinets.

"But, that aside, it sounds to me that Ted has paid you an enormous compliment," Stanley stated. "He's telling you that this is important to the company. In fact, it's so important that he'd rather entrust it to you than entrust it to someone with more expertise. Have you thought of that?"

"I have," Guy replied, looking down at the woven green-and-tan rug under his feet. He felt a twinge of guilt, because he had repaid Ted's vote of confidence in him with little more than complaining.

"So here's my question," Stanley said, his voice causing Guy's gaze to snap back up. "Are you a little too scared to see the facts before your eyes?"

Immediately, Guy realized that his neighbor had hit the nail on the head. "You're right, Stanley," he agreed. "This scares me. I'm afraid I'll mess it up. I'm afraid I'll let Ted down, I'll let the company down, and I'll lose Ted's respect."

"Well, there's nothing wrong with admitting to being scared," Stanley replied. As he continued, his eyes took on an unfocused look, as though he were witnessing a scene in another time and place. "Most people get themselves in trouble when they're too scared to admit they're scared. Then they go diving into trouble with their eyes closed."

Guy thought about that for a moment as he gazed around the room, which displayed decades' worth of memorabilia that Stanley had collected from countries around the world. "You know, Stanley, I feel silly telling someone like you that I'm scared. You've captained ships at sea. You've led men into battle. I remember you telling me about that rescue in the Philippines, with the fishing boat in the typhoon. It was frightening to hear the story. I can't imagine how frightening it was to be there."

"That was pretty hairy, I admit," Stanley said with a shrug, his eyes focusing on Guy once again. "On the other hand, at every minute of that operation I knew exactly what I needed to do in order for us to succeed. The whole crew had done rescue-training drills many times over. So, yes, I was always aware during that mission that something bad might happen. But that wasn't the most scared I'd ever felt in the Navy."

Guy laughed at the thought. "You've had a more dangerous situation that you've never told me about?"

"No," Stanley replied, leaning back in his armchair and crossing his ankles. "Nothing like that. Even during battles and storms, I could always count on my training to help me handle my emotions. But I felt most scared in the Navy when I was handed a huge responsibility that I had never trained for. *That* scared me. I was unprepared and yet all these people were counting on me to not mess up. I felt like I couldn't recognize a threat if it were staring me in the face."

"That describes me right now with this project," Guy told the other man. "It feels like I'm walking into a minefield."

Stanley stood up. "Good. I've got something in the basement I'd like to show you. It's a project I don't think I've ever mentioned before."

CHAPTER 6

To Build a Boat

Stanley led Guy downstairs and stopped in front of a shelf lined with cardboard document boxes, some of which were yellowed with age. After skimming their labels for a few moments, Stanley pulled down a box bearing the name "*U.S.S. Constellation*" and set it gently onto his workbench.

"I don't know why I keep all these old things," he muttered as he rifled through the box's contents. "Well, maybe I keep them all so I can do what I'm doing right now."

Soon, Stanley removed a heavy blue portfolio from the box and laid it flat on the workbench. It contained a set of old black-and-white photographs that showed an aircraft carrier being pulled apart and dismantled, step-by-step. Workers with blowtorches cut huge holes in the metal plating. Sections of decking were peeled back like skin on an orange. Cranes lifted huge guns out of their emplacements, leaving hollowed-out skeletal sockets. Even to Guy's untrained eye, it was clear that the ship was in the process of being stripped to its bare bones.

Stanley turned a page to reveal a full color photo of the *U.S.S. Constellation*. "After Vietnam, the Navy needed to refit its entire fleet of aircraft carriers," he explained. "They had seen so much service they were worn out. Time and technology had passed them by, too. So everything on board had to be replaced—engines, electrical systems, navigation systems, flight decks, guns, even the galleys and the toilets. Everything. It was a massive undertaking, and the *Constellation* was the first aircraft carrier in the fleet to get the full treatment."

"You worked on this?" Guy guessed, turning the pages of photographs.

"I *ran* it," Stanley clarified. "I was the Commanding Officer in charge. It took us three years to get it done, right here at the Philadelphia Naval Yard. At the time, it was the biggest ship overhaul in the history of the U.S. Navy. From stem to stern, the whole project was my responsibility."

Guy flipped through more photographs, his respect for his neighbor growing with each page. "I had no idea, Stanley."

"You want to talk about being scared?" Stanley asked with a chuckle. "I didn't know anything about shipbuilding when I showed up on the first day. I had 30 different unions in the civilian construction trades working under me, and I had no background in any of those trades. I didn't know squat about union contracts or labor relations. I had to learn how to requisition construction materials, read the engineering diagrams, inspect the work, and resolve labor disputes all along the way."

Stanley slid the box closer to him and unfolded a packet of blueprints. The paper at the edges was beginning to crumble from age.

"Not one of these designs turned out the way it was planned," Stanley commented. "A refit of this size had never been done before, so the mistakes kept piling on top of each other. We had to go through one engineering workaround and design amendment after another. And each one had to be sent up the line for approval. Every day was another battle to stay on time and under budget." He refolded the blueprints and returned them to the box.

Guy turned around to lean against the workbench. "So here's the obvious question," he said. "Why did the Navy take the risk of giving you this job? Shouldn't they have gotten another officer with shipbuilding experience? Weren't there other people who had managed refits on smaller ships?"

Stanley smiled as he began to gather up the pile of photos and papers. "The Admiral who gave me this assignment trusted me," he explained. "That's it. He knew I could lead."

"And he thought that made you a better person for the job than someone else with more experience?" Guy questioned, even though he was sure he already knew what the answer would be.

Stanley stopped repacking the document box to stare straight at Guy. "You've heard me say before that management is about stuff—leadership is about people. I learned that from the Admiral. He lived and breathed that idea. He wanted a leader at the top, not a manager."

Stanley looked down and examined the photo on the top of the stack he held. It showed a group of workers wearing welding helmets. "I learned over time that overhauling aircraft carriers is not about the ship, even though one weighs 80,000 tons. The overhaul was about people. People determined how that job got done."

Guy was silent for a moment as he processed what he had just heard. That was one of the many things he liked about his neighbor: Stanley never *gave* him the answers. Instead, he made sure that Guy thought through the issues at hand and arrived at an applicable conclusion himself. Finally, Guy spoke. "The Admiral assumed you don't need to be a shipbuilder in order to lead shipbuilders."

"Exactly," Stanley said, sounding like a teacher praising a star pupil. "We had so much shipbuilding expertise at the Naval Yard that the Admiral didn't need one more expert builder at the head of the project. He wanted someone who could lead. I had 20 years in the service at the time, and he figured I was ready."

"I think I see what you're getting at," Guy mused.

"Do you?" Stanley asked as he returned the final photos and papers to the box. "Because, I have to tell you, I did not welcome this assignment at all. After 20 years, retirement was an option for me. I was looking forward to settling down, maybe teaching at Annapolis or doing leadership training out in San Diego." He laughed and shook his head.

"Instead, I had to go to this little trailer at the Naval Yard every day for three years. It was hot in the summer, cold in the winter, and there I was, with no idea how to build a rowboat, much less rebuild an aircraft carrier. I was completely unqualified for every single job under my direction. Not one person had anything to learn from me in terms of technical or operational know-how. But we got it done."

"So what was the secret?" Guy asked, hoping against hope for a magical solution to his own problems. "How can you lead when you don't know about the work to be done?"

"You start with your leadership philosophy," Stanley said as he replaced the lid on the *Constellation* document box. "That's one thing I know you've done before. You tell your people what they can expect from you, and what you expect from them."

"That's a problem," Guy muttered. "How can I do that when the team members aren't employees who report to me?"

"Well, carry that box upstairs for me, and I'll tell you in the comfort of my study," Stanley replied. "You've got a team made up of people from mostly other companies, right?" Stanley asked as he ushered Guy through the basement door and turned out the lights.

As the two men made their way up the staircase, Guy explained that even the ones who worked for Argosy, like Nigel and Mike Andrews, didn't report directly to him.

"This is usually the case whenever there's a complex task to be tackled," Stanley said. He held up a finger. "Wait just a minute, okay?" he asked as he disappeared into the kitchen. In a moment, he was back with two opened bottles of beer. He set one on top of the document box Guy was holding, and then resumed what he had been saying as he led the way back to the study.

"As the leader, you have to assume that the project is no one's first priority except your own. So you have to bring everyone in, sit them down, and let them know your leadership philosophy—but as their colleague, not as their boss. Then you figure out the action steps as a team, so you have buy-in from everyone. Each one of your team members has to feel a part of the whole process."

Guy was listening intently as he took a seat across from his neighbor and set the *Constellation* box on the coffee table between them. "Ted says this is the kind of project where no one has the answer, but everyone has a piece of the answer."

"Ted's right," Stanley said. He grew animated at the thought. "That's buy-in. Without it, some won't contribute. And because it's a collaboration, you have no power to force them to contribute. So let's say there's a team member who has a piece of the answer, but he's distracted by his other responsibilities. He's not sure of the direction you're leading. He thinks you haven't brought him in on the process. So he sits back and doesn't contribute."

"I've seen that before," Guy replied after taking a sip of his beer. "Heck, I've even *been* one of those people. I get turned off by the process so I pull back and adopt a wait-and-see attitude. But I can see that when you're a leader and that happens, you're sunk." Guy glanced briefly at a model submarine on one of Stanley's bookshelves, then continued. "That person has got a piece of your answer and he's not in the game. Unfortunately, I think it happens all the time."

Stanley nodded his head. "It does. So you need to reach out to anyone you see who's doing that," he said. "You need to really get to know what motivates each individual on the team, because some of your team members are going to respond to challenges and setbacks by withdrawing and hoping things will take care of themselves. When a team starts to drift like that, it's a disaster waiting to happen."

Stanley set his beer down on a coaster and reopened the box containing the *Constellation* documents. "So maybe you shouldn't feel so bad about being scared."

Stanley paused and smiled to make sure Guy knew he was kidding. "A little earlier you mentioned that fishing boat rescue in the Philippines. When I think back on that day, I don't think it required very much from me in the way of leadership. Every crewmember followed his training, and the result was that we saved two dozen lives." Stanley said this with a knowing smile. "Part of the reason why I took so much pride in my crew was that I knew they could have done the whole operation without me, without any Captain. They were so well trained that they hardly needed any leadership at all that day."

Stanley gestured with the lid of the *Constellation* box, which was still in his hands. "But at this level of work, when teams of people from different organizations need to come together and produce a result that's never been done before, leadership is everything. Nothing good happens without leadership."

After spending a few seconds digging into the box, Stanley showed Guy some of his planning documents from the *Constellation* refit. He explained how he started each phase by breaking down the project into terms that everyone involved could see and understand, regardless of expertise. He worked with the teams to develop a series of SMART goals—which, he said, stands for Specific, Measurable, Agreed upon, Realistic and Trackable. According to Stanley, leaders have to make sure every task meets all five criteria or it risks falling through the cracks between the team members' areas of expertise.

"When you go over the SMART goals," Stanley said as he scanned a creased typewritten sheet, "you find pretty quickly that the *process* of planning is more important than the plan itself. I know that sounds strange, but it's true in cases where people are coming together from different disciplines. The common language of the SMART goals is what keeps everyone contributing to solutions for problems that you never anticipated. It keeps everyone in the game and it helps resolve conflicts."

Guy took another sip of beer, then turned the bottle around in his hands for a few moments. "I'm not sure I understand that part," he admitted.

"Well, let me elaborate a little bit, because this is important," Stanley replied. "As I said, the design specifications were often way off, and when we came across a problem area, we had to stop work, look at it, and come up with a quick fix." He shook his head. "Even a tiny problem could hold up progress on a whole section of the ship. Sometimes I'd end up dealing with an angry tradesman with 30 years of experience in shipbuilding, telling me I didn't know what I was doing."

Guy raised his eyebrows as he thought about what his neighbor must have felt like in that situation. "What would you say to him?"

"I'd tell him he was right," Stanley said, chuckling. "After all, it was usually true, and more importantly, it would usually calm the other guy down. Then I'd get everyone together to refine the nature of the problem and propose solutions with the SMART process."

Stanley leaned forward to retrieve his beer from the coffee table. "I remember in one case a master shipbuilder was swearing up and down that this one problem was physically impossible to solve. And we got together with the SMART process and we found a workaround. It was ugly as sin, but it worked."

"Right," Guy said as he processed what he had just heard. "The shipbuilder thought you had an unsolvable physical problem. But the solution involved getting more people involved."

Stanley nodded as he took a drink. "With 30 trades and dozens of contractors working on that project, there were constant disputes and conflicts," he recounted. "Your instinct, anyone's instinct, is to push conflicts aside and hope they'll go away. But the leader's role demands the moral courage to address conflict." Stanley leaned back in his chair as he let that last thought sink in.

"Partly that's because if the leader doesn't address conflict, no one else will," he continued. "But mainly it's because the project won't succeed if conflicts go unaddressed. Whenever bad things happen, it's usually because there was a lack of leadership somewhere along the line. I learned that, too."

Stanley put the lid on the *Constellation* box and slid it toward the edge of the coffee table. "You know, Guy, until I worked on the *Constellation*, I had never really appreciated the importance of moral courage in a leader," he said as he stood.

Guy followed suit, smoothing out the creases in his slacks.

"Honestly, I learned more and grew more as a person from that job than from anything else I've ever done," Stanley admitted as the two men walked toward the front door. "Believe me, this project you're facing feels overwhelming now. But I predict that once you are done with it, you will feel like you can handle anything. That is, unless you still intend to tell Ted you don't want to do it."

Guy smiled. "This is probably why Ted told me I should come talk to you."

"I know you admire Ted," Stanley said as they made their way onto the porch. The soft sound of crickets surrounded them. "You should understand that for him this project has already started. Your reluctance to lead is a practical problem he holds himself accountable for."

Stanley paused and looked straight at Guy. "He knows you doubt his judgment on this, but he hasn't taken it personally, has he? He hasn't told you that you must do it. He hasn't tried to shame you or bully you. Instead, he asked himself, *How can I motivate Guy to take a clearer look at this project? I think I'll tell him to go talk to Stanley.* That's leadership. I don't think Ted is desperate, Guy. I think he's wiser than you may think."

"I'm sure that's true," Guy replied, the words coming slowly. His mind reeled for a moment. Was Ted Stone really that smart?

Stanley put his hand on Guy's shoulder. "So what do you think? Are you ready to go build yourself a boat?"

Ted's plan had worked. Guy felt ready to lead.

PART TWO

CHAPTER 7

Introductions and Ideas

The first meeting of the wave-and-pay working group was held in a hotel conference room near Argosy's offices. Guy arrived to find a dozen people gathered around the long polished-wood table, which held a few trays of muffins, pastries, and bagels. Apparently, the trains from New York and Washington had been delayed that morning, so some of the team members had arrived late and there had been little time to socialize prior to the start of the meeting.

Since Guy was leading the project (even though the idea still made him more than a little nervous), he spoke first to welcome everyone and asked that each person in the room introduce themselves.

Most of the meeting's attendees turned out to be technical advisers from CellMobile and MegaMart. Also present were MegaMart's retail innovation director, Robert Durham, and one of CellMobile's vice presidents, Margaret Hsei. Besides Guy himself, the group was rounded out by his colleagues from Argosy:

Linda, Nigel, and Mike Andrews, Argosy's chief of product marketing.

Looking around at the oval of faces in front of him, Guy decided to kick things off by addressing his role in the group.

"We're all here because we've been asked to propose a retail system that marries mobile payments with in-store mobile promotions and marketing," he began. "Wave-and-pay is the critical piece in the puzzle. Our task is to come up with a recommended path for making this retail system a reality. We need to produce a consensus document that would be the basis for our companies to begin a formal three-way partnership."

Everyone listened to Guy intently, except Mike Andrews, who was picking at his blueberry muffin.

So far, so good...I guess, Guy thought as he forged ahead.

"I should acknowledge right away that I personally don't know that much about mobile phones or retail management, so I can't really see all the challenges in front of us, in terms of software, communications, engineering, and retail systems," he admitted, striving to keep his voice strong and confident. He didn't want these people to make incorrect assumptions regarding his expertise, but it was also imperative that they saw—and continued to see—him as a leader. "But all of you know certain pieces of this picture very well. So my job is to bring us all together and move us forward toward a common goal."

Guy reached down to open a document on his laptop, which was connected to a digital projector. Almost in unison, all of the heads around the conference table swiveled to look at a timeline of wave-and-pay progress around the world, including parking meters in Serbia and soda machines in Japan.

"I've been doing a lot of reading about wave-and-pay in the past few weeks," Guy shared as the group studied the timeline. "As you can see, it's a proven concept in most developed countries, but not in the U.S. That tells me that we're not facing a technical problem here. It's a *people* problem. And until today, I don't think the right group of people in the U.S. has ever gotten together with a commitment to make wave-and-pay work."

Guy noticed a few thoughtful nods as he clicked to the next page in his presentation. It read, "Objective: A new world retail industry standard."

"Our objective," Guy stated, "is to set the industry standard for wave-and-pay in the U.S. and around the world. That means we need to identify one integrated, interoperable system that is acceptable to all three of our companies." He stepped sideways, partially blocking the text on the screen. It was important that everyone pay attention to what he was about to say.

"As you know, this is a huge task. And we need to do it in a short period of time so we can get a jump on the competition. In just *ten weeks* we will identify a consensus system and produce a document that explains why we think this system is the best way to go."

Guy looked around the table, trying to make eye contact with everyone. While some faces were difficult to read, he thought he saw several expressions of determination and even excitement. It

was a relief that no one seemed to be daunted by the timeline…
at least not yet.

Satisfied that everyone understood the magnitude of what
they were undertaking, Guy returned to his laptop and clicked
to the next overhead page: "SMART Goals."

"Now, why do I say we face a people problem and not a technical problem?" Guy asked. "Because the technology already ex-
ists. It's working in other countries. What we need is a business
strategy, a people strategy, for bringing wave-and-pay to the U.S.
My job is to lead us by defining our work in a series of SMART
goals."

Guy paused to take a sip of his coffee—it was lukewarm by
this point—then explained the concept Stanley had shared with
him. "SMART goals are ones that meet five criteria: Specific.
Measurable. Agreed upon. Realistic. Trackable."

Guy saw Robert Durham, MegaMart's retail innovation director, writing down each word, and couldn't suppress a small
smile. *Thanks, Stanley—you're already helping us get off to a good
start*, he thought.

Now it was time to bring everyone else into the discussion.
Guy turned off the projector and asked the group for ideas on
what they would consider the essential activities required to
meet their objective in ten weeks.

Without hesitation, one of the engineers from CellMobile
suggested a four-step technical plan that would examine and test
the competing international standards for wireless communication frequencies and encoding systems. By the time the young

man had finished speaking, Guy was completely confused. Between the technical jargon and the engineer's fast pace, Guy knew he'd be fortunate if he had correctly understood half of what had been said. And based on a few other bewildered expressions, he wasn't the only one.

Margaret, CellMobile's team leader, must have noticed that part of the group was already lost. She gave a strained grin and tried to explain. "If CellMobile phones are going to function like credit cards in MegaMart stores, then I think we should start by agreeing on certain technical specifications with MegaMart. Each phone will need to communicate with MegaMart's cash register, make a secure transfer of account information, and then confirm the transaction."

"So," Guy said, trying to simplify the idea further, "wave-and-pay is a three-step communication task for the phone. It has to read the total on the register, transfer the funds, and confirm the transaction. Is that it?"

"There's more to it than that," interjected one of the MegaMart people whose name escaped Guy at the moment. "Every credit or debit transaction has twelve steps, not three. It starts with application selection, then initiating application processing—"

This time Robert Durham interrupted. "I think each of those twelve steps fit under one or the other of the three headings that Guy proposed," he said, his palm facing outward in a placating gesture. "For our planning purposes, why don't we use those three steps: read, transfer, confirm."

Guy heaved a quick inward sigh of relief, thankful that Robert had helped to keep the meeting from derailing less than half an hour in. He knew that at this point, it was important to stay focused on the big picture. The details could, and would, come into play later.

Nigel—wearing a blue-and-green-plaid bowtie today—jumped in with his pet subject, mobile marketing. "We may need a fourth step for electronic coupons and loyalty points," he asserted. "Wave-and-pay needs to help shoppers save money and improve their experience or they won't use it. It takes mobile sales and incentives to get more CellMobile customers shopping at MegaMart and more MegaMart customers signing up with CellMobile." Nigel's enthusiasm for the idea elicited smiles all around.

"When I walk into a MegaMart," Nigel continued, practically bouncing up and down in his seat, "a wireless system will track my phone through the store. It will retrieve and display electronic coupons and special offers related to my MegaMart purchasing history. Then all the savings I captured on my phone need to be applied to my bill automatically when I make the wave-and-pay move at the register. "

"So should we call it four factors?" Guy asked, looking around the table for consensus. "Read the register, transfer discounts, transfer the payment, confirm the transaction." As he spoke, he jotted down each step on a legal pad.

"That's exactly how paper coupons work," the MegaMart technician who had spoken earlier commented. "They're deducted from the register total after all the purchases have been rung up."

Guy was relieved to arrive at such a simple conclusion regarding what each wave-and-pay transaction entailed. But as he clicked his pen closed, he wondered why the technician had brought up the 12-step technical process to begin with. He supposed that the man was simply fixated on his own area of responsibility and didn't want it to be neglected.

A 90-minute discussion followed as the group weighed upsides and downsides of wave-and-pay systems in Europe and Asia. CellMobile's team raised concerns about how some systems drain too much power from mobile phone batteries. MegaMart's team expressed doubts about software reliability and the per-store cost of hardware. Nigel gave his best guesses as to which wireless in-store promotions produced the most revenue.

But despite the amount of expertise that was gathered around the conference table, the gaps in collective knowledge became clear as the discussion went on. Ted had *definitely* been right. Everyone had bits and pieces of information to contribute, but no one in the room had a complete vision of the answer.

After listening and asking questions all morning, Guy felt that he knew what needed to happen in order for everyone to move forward. He stood up to make sure that he had everyone's attention, then proposed that the group's first task be to identify all the competing wireless protocols that allow the phone to accept coupons and work with wave-and-pay. Specifically, CellMobile would organize the research on phone design, while

MegaMart would do the same for point-of-sale devices. Nigel and Mike agreed to assemble information on wireless in-store marketing.

"I know that you've all done a lot of this research already," Guy told the group. "But now we need to be more thorough, and we have to make our research intelligible to each other." He raised his eyebrows and smiled, and was rewarded with a few scattered chuckles. They all knew that what Guy had just asked for was much easier said than done.

"Try to keep in mind the 'measurable' factor in the SMART goals," Guy continued. "I'd like to ask everyone to organize the research in a format that even I can understand." Almost everyone laughed this time. "For example, please don't tell me that something is high-frequency or ultra-high-frequency without spelling out the advantages and disadvantages relating to our objective—a mobile commerce world standard."

Everyone agreed that organizing, simplifying, and sharing research would be their first objective, and that it needed to be complete in two weeks. By week four, the team decided, these options would have to be narrowed down to the best three. Then by week six, CellMobile and MegaMart would have to provide their assessments on how well each of the three options would operate within their respective internal systems. By week eight, the group would arrive at its consensus recommendation. The report would be drafted and approved by week ten.

To Guy's pleasant surprise, all of this discussion was over by lunchtime, and he was satisfied that everyone at the table had one or more SMART assignments for the week two meeting. Before the group scattered, though, Guy had one more item of business to address. He rifled through his briefcase and pulled out a sheet of paper that contained an abridged version of his personal leadership philosophy.

Glancing at the paper periodically to make sure he wasn't skipping anything, Guy stuck to the main points of the "PLP" he had developed during the Eaton/Argosy merger several years ago. With this group of important collaborators, he made sure to put each point in the form of a polite request rather than a demand: "Please propose solutions when you point out problems. Please let everyone know if something you're responsible for will be late. Let's keep our senses of humor. Let's learn from mistakes. Let's not gossip. Let's be on time."

As Guy unplugged his laptop and packed up his other belongings a few minutes later, a feeling of excitement welled up in him. He indulged himself in one more glance at his project planner before putting it into his briefcase. It all looked very tidy: three partnering companies, three sets of tasks, each set broken down into neat columns.

The lessons he had learned from Stanley really had been invaluable, Guy reflected. Every time he had spoken at the meeting, he had done his best to shift the subject of conversation away from technology and toward the team members and their tasks. He kept putting people ahead of "stuff," and it had worked like a charm.

Maybe this leadership task wasn't so impossible after all.

Chapter 8

Introductions, Questions, and Concerns

As the meeting broke up, Guy stood near the conference room's door in something of a reception line as members of the CellMobile and MegaMart teams approached him and introduced themselves personally. Robert Durham, a beefy, effusive man who headed the MegaMart team, grabbed Guy's hand and thanked him for leading the meeting. Robert looked to be in his mid-to-late thirties, Guy's own age.

"I've been hoping for years that retail would start moving in this direction," Robert confided. "We've been taking a beating from online competition. This is the way to catch up and make retail shopping faster and more fun."

"Fast and fun sounds good," Guy replied. He felt self-conscious for a moment, since he liked shopping online and rarely ever visited a MegaMart store. "Fast and fun is a good approach for this working group, too. Let's get this done fast and let's have fun along the way."

As they chatted, Guy learned that Robert's first job with MegaMart had been as a computer programmer. He then moved up to systems analyst before his latest promotion, two years earlier, to director level. Most of his work with MegaMart had involved automated inventory control. Recently, Robert said, he had completed a major project aimed at limiting out-of-stock items by tracking consumer habits and sales patterns in stores around the world.

"That sounds like an amazing project," Guy replied, meaning it. "Did you have to do a lot of traveling?"

"I never left my cubicle!" Robert said with evident pride. "It's all data crunching with algorithms. The patterns emerged from the math." Robert, who was clearly enthused by his topic, explained how MegaMart uses automated systems to track all items at its thousands of stores, every minute around the clock and around the world. Gesticulating frequently, he described how he had analyzed inventory data for stores according to location code numbers, often unaware of whether he was calculating the supply needs for a store in Chicago or in Shanghai.

"Our goal with that project was to make sure no store would ever be out-of-stock on any item for more than 24 hours," Robert concluded. "We run a goal-oriented shop, very results-focused. I think that's why I liked your SMART planning approach so much. It's very...smart." He gave a weak chuckle.

"Did Frank and Vera also work on that project?" Guy wanted to know more about the other two MegaMart team members that Robert brought with him. Compared to Robert, neither had said very much during the meeting.

"Oh, no," Robert replied. "I've never worked with either of them before. Frank is a specialist in point-of-sale technology, as you might have guessed from all that talk about 12-step transactions."

Guy nodded, pleased that he had been correct in assuming that the man had gone into so much detail because he had simply been focusing on his own area of responsibility.

"Vera is from retail promotions," Robert continued. "She works on pricing strategies by studying my purchase pattern reports. Both of them use data from my office to do their jobs, so that's why I was made team leader for this project. Inventory, point-of-purchase, promotions—all three functions need to work seamlessly, so our big concern will always be about systems compatibility."

After his explanation, Robert excused himself to check train schedules with his team members. That gave Guy a chance to catch up with Linda, who had been chatting up Margaret, the CellMobile vice president.

"I see a few problems so far," Linda muttered, motioning Guy over to an alcove in the hallway. "Margaret is worried that MegaMart hasn't been very responsive in the past week. She and a few other techies from CellMobile tried reaching out to them and they couldn't get any information."

Guy was feeling optimistic after talking to Robert. "I think that will change now that we've all gotten together."

Linda stirred her coffee, causing steam to rise from the cup. "Margaret would also like to know what's up with Mike Andrews. He seems mentally checked out, and we've barely gotten started."

Guy nodded, recalling how Mike had been picking at his muffin while the rest of the group had listened intently to Guy's introduction. And as things had progressed, Mike had contributed nothing to the meeting. He seemed to be only half-listening to the discussion, and had raced out the door the minute it was over. "You're right. I'll talk to him," Guy promised. "But first, I want to check in with the MegaMart team one more time. Margaret's concerns have me wondering about something."

Robert Durham was getting ready to leave when Guy rejoined him. "Before you go, Robert, I wanted to ask your advice on something. If you were in my shoes, what would you say I should look out for? What are the potential sticking points, as you see them?"

Robert shrugged. "I don't see any, Guy. Why do you ask?"

"I'm wondering, for instance, if proprietary systems might give us some problems. Secret data or software MegaMart can't share. It would be good to know in advance what we might need to steer around."

Guy waited, hoping that Robert might offer an explanation as to why his team had ignored CellMobile's information requests. To his chagrin, Robert didn't take the bait.

"We're an open book," Robert said, spreading his arms as if to prove he wasn't hiding anything. "We have more than 20,000 suppliers and we treat them like our partners. We give them all our technical specs and encourage them to make their inventory and revenue systems compatible with ours. Every aspect of our company has been written about in the newspapers and studied in business schools a dozen times over. You'll find secrecy is the least of your worries with us."

Robert leaned in, his voice pitched low. "CellMobile, though, might be a different story."

Guy raised an eyebrow. "Why is that?"

"It's the nature of the industry," Robert replied. He rolled his eyes. "Telecommunications has lots more trade secrets than retail. Just ask anyone."

The two shook hands and promised to stay in touch over the coming two weeks. Robert's answer left Guy with the sense that maybe Margaret wasn't telling everything she knew. If MegaMart had seemed unforthcoming to her, maybe it was CellMobile's fault and she didn't even see it.

Down in the hotel lobby, Guy caught up with Mike Andrews, who was finishing a conversation on his cell phone. He turned and started walking toward the exit when he saw Guy approach. "I've got no time, Guy," he called over his shoulder. "I need to get back to the office."

With a few quick steps, Guy caught up and walked alongside the other man. "When would be a better time, Mike?"

"I don't know," Mike muttered, chewing his bottom lip. He averted his gaze, choosing to stare at a potted palm instead of

Guy. "I've got paying clients all backed up into the middle of next week."

Guy knew he couldn't let Mike off the hook that easily. If Mike didn't pull his weight, the whole project might get derailed. At the very least, the other team members' lives would be a whole lot harder. "I'd like to ask you about the items you're responsible for two weeks from now."

"Can you talk to Nigel about that?" Mike hedged as he pulled open the hotel lobby's door. "You ran a good meeting today, and I think there's really something to this wave-and-pay thing. But I'm tied up with clients. We've got bills to pay this month, you know?"

"Maybe if…"

"I've gotta make another call, Guy," Mike interrupted. "Please take your questions to Nigel for now. That's what he's paid for." He suddenly seemed embarrassed by his own abruptness. "Oh, and congratulations. That was a great meeting." Mike strode away and left Guy standing alone on the sidewalk.

CHAPTER 9

Talk about Teamwork

A little over one week later, Linda Hutchinson had once again parked herself in Guy's office to talk about the Flavor Burst social media campaign. A young woman named Taylor was managing the project's startup, and Linda was concerned that some of the internal deadlines were beginning to slip.

"She's really anxious to please you, Guy," Linda pointed out, "but her youth and inexperience are beginning to show."

"I promised you I would step back," Guy responded, scanning his email inbox out of the corner of his eye. "Now I'm wondering if that's the right move for this project. I built in a lot of padding in the internal deadlines. How much padding are we going to let Taylor burn through before we reach in and start telling her what to do?"

"This is an update, nothing more," Linda clarified. "There is no 'we' about this. You promised you'd stay out of it, and I'm going to hold you to it."

Guy double-clicked a subject line, opening the email in a separate window. "Tell Taylor that if she wants my advice on something she should come to me and ask for it," he said. "Otherwise I'm not going to mention it to her."

"You're learning," observed Linda with a smile. "I really appreciate your restraint."

Guy smiled too. They both knew that not so long ago, the same comment would have been sarcastic instead of sincere.

"I don't have the time and attention to spare," Guy admitted. It was the cold, hard truth. "The week two meeting of wave-and-pay is on Friday and I'm still not prepared." He pointed to a stack of reading on a side table in his office.

"Well, good luck with that," Linda said as she got up to leave.

Later in the day as he made his way down the hallway, Guy bumped into Ted Stone, who was at the Eaton/Argosy offices for an afternoon meeting.

"I haven't had a chance to ask you about MegaMart and CellMobile," Ted exclaimed. "You're meeting again in the next couple of days?"

"That's right. And everything's going great," Guy replied. "We've got our plan, and we're all following through on it." Guy didn't want to sound boastful, but aside from his concerns about Mike's lack of interest in the project, he was feeling very good about the direction of the working group.

"Sounds promising," Ted commended. "Actually, while I'm here, why don't we sit down in your office for a few minutes so that you can give me the rundown?"

After the two men were seated, Ted asked for details. Guy explained that in the first meeting, he made sure that each team member had been given clear and concise expectations. Now there was a ten-week plan built around the SMART goal system.

"Everyone knows their roles," Guy confirmed with a smile. "MegaMart and CellMobile sent us top-notch people and they are really excited about this project."

"They told you that?" Ted asked. He sounded somewhat skeptical.

"Yes, they did," Guy replied. He wondered where Ted's doubts were coming from. "Robert, the retail innovation director from MegaMart, couldn't stop talking about how wave-and-pay is the future and how we're the ones who are going to make it happen."

"So your team members all know what they've got to bring to Friday's meeting? And you're not concerned at all?"

Ted still had a dubious look on his face, and it was starting to make Guy feel self-conscious. He shifted in his seat.

"As far as I know, everyone has their work cut out for them between our last meeting and Friday, and they'll follow through," Guy said. He instantly regretted his answer and winced inwardly.

"As far as you know?" Ted asked, pouncing on Guy's choice of words. "So you're not in touch with them? You're not checking in with them, the way I'm checking in with you right now?"

Feeling ill at ease, Guy rolled a pen back and forth on his desk calendar. "No, I'm expecting that they will do what they said they would do," he responded. "We agreed on the agenda for the next meeting. It was clear to everyone what they needed to do in order to stay with the plan."

He didn't tell Ted that he'd been trying to get Robert Durham on the phone to ask him a question about MegaMart, and that his calls to Robert had gone unreturned.

"Okay, so you're sure you know what's going to happen at the next meeting, right?" Ted was being persistent.

Guy sighed. He was done with defending his decisions, especially since he now suspected they hadn't been as wise as he thought. "Ted, tell me what I'm missing. What should I be doing that I'm not doing?"

"You said that you trust your people," Ted said. He stroked his chin for a moment. "That's good. But when I heard that, I wondered if you'd missed a step. I mean to say that you've worked out a plan with them, laid out the goals, and that's fine as far as it goes. That's the crucial first step. But now I hear you saying you trust them to live up to your expectations."

"I've *got* to trust them," Guy replied, fiddling with the pen again. "That's the challenge, I thought. It's not like I can jump in and tell them how to do their work, even if I wanted to."

Ted smiled and shook his head. "That's not what I'm talking about," he said. "If you're not in touch with the team members, then you still don't know them very well. When I say you might have missed a step, I mean that I'm concerned that you haven't built a team yet, that you haven't begun building it."

Despite his respect for his boss, Guy was beginning to feel exasperated. "There's a dozen people around that table, Ted."

"I'm talking about the key people," Ted replied. He ignored the edge that had crept into Guy's voice. "I mean Robert, MegaMart's lead person, and Margaret, the V.P. from CellMobile. You've gotten to know Nigel, but you've never worked with Mike from product marketing before. I'm saying that you need to know what's going on with these people so that your expectations of them are realistic. Does that make sense?"

"Sure."

"It's usually not an easy lesson to learn, but the truth is that everyone means something different when they respond to a question with 'yes,' 'no,' or 'maybe,'" Ted explained. "When Margaret from CellMobile says she'll do something, does that mean she'll do it, or that she's going to try, or that she hopes to do it? That's what you have to know about each team member if you're going to lead effectively, and what I hear you saying is that you're taking each member's word at face value. I'm suggesting to you that it's dangerous to do that."

Already, Guy felt guilty for losing his patience, because Ted had brought up a very good point. "It's funny you mention Mike from product marketing," he said. "I stopped by yesterday to ask him a question, and I did check in with him. I asked how it was going for his Friday meeting deliverables, and he got a little annoyed with me. Overall, I'd say he's not very enthusiastic about this project."

"Yeah, that's Mike," said Ted with a shrug. "He's from the old school, where the clients pay us at an hourly rate, and our best efforts are reserved for the highest-paying clients. The idea of partnering on a project like this, on spec, is pretty alien to him. He probably complained to you about how he's got to tend to his paying clients first."

"Something like that." Guy was impressed by how accurate Ted's guess was. He put the pen down and made a conscious effort to keep his hands still on the desk.

"Listen, Mike is very important to this firm," Ted said, leaning back and crossing his ankles. "He has been for years. He has done more than anyone here to hold on to our most valuable clients and keep them happy."

Guy nodded. "I don't doubt it. But how did he wind up in this group when he obviously doesn't want to be a part of it?"

A sly smile spread across Ted's face. "Besides the fact that he really knows marketing, I put him with you so he could see the writing on the wall. We're going to be doing more and more things like this. I can't leave Mike out of the company's future."

Sounds like Mike is in for a rude awakening, Guy thought.

Ted chuckled as though reading Guy's mind. Then he became serious again. "And that's what I was talking about when I brought up building a team. Now that you know this about Mike, you'll handle him accordingly. But what about Robert and Margaret? Do you know the same sort of things about them?

How did they get where they are? How do they handle their responsibilities?"

Ted looked Guy in the eyes. "Once you really understand each member of your team on that level, then you can say that you've *really* built a team."

"I hear you," Guy replied. Mentally, he was already reviewing the implications of what he had just learned from Ted, and decided to be totally honest about his concerns.

"Robert, at MegaMart, is a problem. I've left him three phone messages because I had a question for him, and I haven't gotten a response. I assumed he's busy, like everyone, but..." Guy trailed off. It was difficult to verbally admit that he had, perhaps, been wrong.

"But you're also learning something about whether you can count on him to be responsive," Ted concluded for Guy. "You may want to talk to him about that. The conversation will help you develop a more credible and predictable relationship. Then you're building a team."

"I get your point, Ted. Thanks."

Ted was silent for a moment, and then his face softened. "Right now, Guy, you are leading without authority and that's the toughest leadership challenge of all," Ted admitted. "I know and you know that you don't have real clout with these people. You're the team leader, but Robert, Margaret, Mike, and Nigel aren't your subordinates. So you need to remember that when you're out of their sight, they're likely to forget all about you and your working group."

Guy couldn't help picking up his pen once again. Ted's words were making him feel increasingly nervous. "That's the feeling I'm getting from Robert."

"I've learned from my own personal experience that the only currency you have as a leader is the quality of your relationships with your group members," Ted responded. "Relationships are important in every workplace situation, but they're especially important when you're leading without authority. Then your relationships are all you've got."

Ted's face brightened at the sound of his own wise words. Guy took this all in for a moment, not sure what to say. If Ted was right—and Guy suspected he was—then Guy was pretty close to not having anything at all when it came to being the working group's leader.

"Hey," said Ted, rising and grabbing his briefcase and overcoat. "You may prove me wrong on Friday. Maybe everyone will come through as promised. But keep in mind that every problem is an occasion for a conversation. Talk to Robert about whether he's getting your phone messages. That's a chance to build some trust. And trust is how you build your team." He nodded to Guy and disappeared into the hallway.

Excuses, Exasperation, and Opposition

Two days before the week two meeting, everyone had filed reports except the MegaMart team members. On Thursday, the day before the meeting, Guy called Robert several times in hopes of receiving an update. But as before, his calls went unanswered and unreturned.

Fortunately, Guy felt a bit more confident in regard to the other group members. Earlier in the week, CellMobile's reports had come in, and Guy and Nigel had gone over them for technical compatibility issues. Mike Andrews was nowhere to be found (which wasn't entirely a surprise), so Guy called Freddie Jencks to come down and offer his perspective. Freddie worked in Mike's office, knew his way around mobile marketing, and had some interesting things to contribute. For the moment, Guy didn't mind that Mike was out of the loop because things were moving forward without any snags.

On the morning of the meeting, an out-of-patience Guy finally made contact with Robert on his cell phone.

"I'm in the 'quiet car' on the train," Robert hissed. "Can't talk."

"Please move to another car," Guy requested, trying not to let his exasperation show in his voice. "Then call me back. I need to get a quick briefing on what you're bringing to the meeting today."

There was no answer before Guy heard the line go dead. He stared at his phone, surprised by Robert's behavior, which was brusque even for someone in the "quiet car." Then his phone buzzed with a text from Robert: "sorry. no report today."

You've got to be kidding me.

An hour later, Robert and his MegaMart team strolled through the conference room door. The CellMobile people had yet to arrive, and Guy used the fortuitous timing to take Robert aside.

Guy was direct. "Can you fill me in on what's happened with your reports before CellMobile gets here?"

"This is all a learning process," Robert said in an apologetic tone. He shrugged. "We looked at everything and realized there are some fundamental issues that Argosy and CellMobile need to hash out before we could offer anything constructive. We think that you both should identify the systems that show the best potential for CellMobile and for Nigel's electronic discount and coupon plans. Then, when we can see what you both consider workable and desirable, we can offer our input."

Robert smiled and leaned back against the wall. Clearly, he thought his explanation was perfectly adequate.

"But that's not what we agreed to," Guy said with a tight smile, which masked his anger. "You're asking us to do all this research without any idea about what MegaMart is willing to spend per store, or what physical obstacles the stores might have to installing these systems."

"I don't think we ever agreed to start costing out things now," Robert replied. He pushed himself off the wall. "Let's not get ahead of ourselves. We will look at what you decide and then give our own assessment. It's really the best way to go."

Guy couldn't help but feel that Robert was patronizing him, but he tried to put a positive spin on what he was asking for nevertheless. "It would be so helpful, though, to have the benefit of your team's expertise," he reasoned. "Some of the systems we're looking at are very expensive. If you can't help us narrow our focus, we might choose a system that MegaMart won't want to pay for."

Robert's gaze slid past Guy and locked on to the coffee maker in the corner of the conference room. "If it's a good system that works, we'll deal with that," he said. "For now, this is the way we prefer to handle it." Then he nodded to Guy, signaling that the conversation was over. He made a beeline for the coffee.

When the CellMobile team arrived, Margaret was ready with a list of questions about the in-store promotion systems Nigel and Freddie had proposed. The technical conversation went over Guy's head after the first few sentences, entering the realm of wavelengths and signal strengths. As Guy observed the reactions of various people around the table, he saw Robert and the other

MegaMart team members taking copious notes and decided that it was a good sign.

Nigel had certainly put a lot of work into his presentation. He walked the group through a series of retail mobile discount systems, each of which required a different type of phone chip. Each phone chip varied in wavelength, range, and cost.

"I prefer the more flexible systems," Nigel said, his gaze flickering around the table. "Experience in Europe shows, however, that they are the most difficult to install and maintain. They also draw the most battery power from phones that interact with them." He tilted his head to one side and pursed his lips as he let everyone consider that drawback.

"How serious is this battery-drain concern?" asked Frank from MegaMart.

"A fast-draining battery for us is like an out-of-stock item for you," explained Margaret. "It makes customers unhappy."

"But we can't restrict the capabilities of a wave-and-pay system just because of battery life, can we?" Frank asked.

Guy didn't give Margaret a chance to respond. "We're looking for common ground right now," he interjected. "We shouldn't start to weigh costs and benefits until the next meeting."

Frank settled back in his chair looking satisfied, but Margaret's brows were drawn down in a "V." Guy could tell she was angry, but his first priority was keeping the meeting on track. He took a sip of his coffee and motioned for Nigel to resume the floor.

As Nigel continued his presentation, he asked the MegaMart team several times if they could shed any light on some of the store design and installation issues he'd uncovered. But Robert and his team offered nothing in response, saying only that they were taking notes and would respond later.

Nigel, whose elf-like face displayed his every emotion, tried and failed to hide his disappointment. A look of chagrin appeared atop his royal-blue bowtie.

Guy decided that the most productive course of action would simply be to move on. "Let's discuss the schedule," he said. "By our next meeting, week four, we are supposed to be ready to narrow our focus to three alternative systems. We're not going to make that deadline unless we get some substantive responses from MegaMart within the next week."

For good measure, Guy fixed Robert with an unblinking stare. From a few seats down, Margaret was doing the same.

Robert clicked his pen open and closed a few times.

Maybe all of this peer pressure is making him uncomfortable after all, Guy mused. *We can only hope it'll light a fire underneath him and his team after this week's disappointment.*

Finally, Robert nodded his head. "Yes, yes," he said. "We will have our first assessments ready a few days before the week four meeting. We'll stay on track."

He made a face that Guy assumed was supposed to be apologetic.

"I think this will prove to be for the best," Robert concluded, directing a smile around the oval table.

Margaret was clearly irritated, and Guy couldn't blame her. Frankly, Robert's reassurances hadn't cut it with him, either.

"Well, we've got a train to catch," Margaret announced. "If we leave now we can all make it home before dinner."

As she rose from her chair, Margaret gave a tightlipped smile and a wave of the hand to Robert and his group members. She shook hands more cordially with Nigel and Freddie and thanked them for their work. And she rolled her eyes at Guy as the two other CellMobile team members preceded her out the door.

Without CellMobile in the room, Nigel felt more comfortable steering some direct questions toward the MegaMart team. But all Robert did was acknowledge that Nigel was raising very good questions and promised to get back to him. Before long, an awkward silence had settled on the room.

"I think we've made all the progress we can today," Guy observed. His voice sounded unnaturally loud, but it did seem to break the group out of its trance. Robert started packing up his things, and the other MegaMart group members followed suit.

Guy caught a moment alone with Robert in the hallway. "You've listed a fourth team member from MegaMart," he prompted. "A retail specialist named Hans? He's missed both meetings so far. We've never met him."

"Hans is the best guy we have in retail tech," Robert replied. "But he's on another assignment, a big project that involves China and Southeast Asia."

Of course he is, Guy thought.

"I'm asking because Nigel and one of the CellMobile people tried to reach him," Guy explained. "Hans has written some articles about wave-and-pay, and they'd like to talk to him."

Robert shook his head. "Sometimes even I have trouble getting Hans's attention," he said, and heaved an exaggerated sigh. "And Hans and I work in the same building! Those calls really should be coming to me. I'll forward the requests to Hans."

That reply gave Guy an opening to finally ask the question he'd been wondering about all day: "Is everything okay with your team?"

Robert seemed a little taken aback. He opened and closed his mouth a few times before responding, and Guy could practically see some of the proverbial wind coming out of his sails.

"I know this isn't ideal," Robert admitted. "But I've found that you can't push the tech people into things, or you get a big mess. They need some patience. If they tell me they don't want to do a report until they see more information from Argosy and CellMobile, I have to accept that."

For the first time, Guy realized how poorly Robert was leading his team. Frank, Vera, and the invisible Hans were doing as they pleased. Meanwhile, Robert merely made excuses for what they did or didn't do. Although Robert had promised to do better by week four, Guy knew it was a promise he could not keep. Preoccupied by his thoughts, he waved goodbye to Robert and returned to the conference room to gather his own belongings.

Later that afternoon, Guy put in a call to Margaret, who was still on the train.

"This high-handed treatment from MegaMart is unbelievable," Margaret said, her frustration coming through loud and clear over the phone line. "We do all the work and *maybe* they'll consider what we've done."

Guy listened. He didn't want to argue with her, especially since he agreed that MegaMart hadn't exactly been an ideal part of the team thus far.

"Everyone back at the office is saying, 'I told you so,'" Margaret continued. "They've all heard how MegaMart likes to play the role of God with its partners."

"Yes, I read that once in *Fortune* magazine," Guy commented.

"My high school Latin kept coming back to me all through the meeting," she said with a wry chuckle. "*Homo proponit, sed Deus disponit.*"

Guy laughed. "What does that mean?"

"Mankind proposes, but God disposes," Margaret replied. "That's what's going on here. We propose and let MegaMart dispose."

"I certainly feel disposed of today," Guy admitted, swiveling his desk chair to face toward his office window. "I'm sure you do, too. The only thing I'd caution you about is that Robert doesn't mean to be high-handed. I think he was very embarrassed."

"He covers it up pretty well if that's true." Margaret was not about to give Robert any breaks.

"He's putting up this front of how MegaMart is choosing to handle things," Guy explained. "I talked to him after the meeting, and it turns out that he has no influence with Frank and Vera. And he can't even get someone named Hans to come to meetings."

Now Margaret laughed. "You're supposed to be making me feel better, Guy," she said. "If that's true about Robert, then things are even worse than I thought."

The conversation left Guy feeling sad and powerless. After he hung up, he stared out at the wintry cityscape while he tried to wrap his brain around the day's events. Earlier that morning, he'd been so excited about the meeting, but it had ended in a fiasco. Each element of the working group was pulling in a different direction. If nothing improved within the next week, Guy felt sure that Margaret would terminate CellMobile's involvement and the whole effort would collapse.

Guy wasn't sure what his next move should be, but he knew he had to do something to salvage this important project.

Assigning Accountability

When Guy pulled up to his house at the end of the day, Melanie's minivan was blocking the driveway. The rear liftgate was open and Stanley was helping Melanie unload an antique dining room set.

"You're here in the nick of time!" Melanie yelled. "Can you and Stanley take all this into the garage? I've got to go check what the girls are up to. It's been too quiet in there for too long." She headed back into the house.

"That's a strong wife you've got," commented Stanley as he took the last chair out of the van. "Smart, too. She was telling me all about how she made a deal on this set."

Guy smiled. "I know! Would you believe that last month Melanie brought home more money than I did with these antiques?" Guy asked. "I've told her that I'm in the wrong business."

"Thinking about retiring early?" Stanley joked.

Guy rubbed a hand back and forth through his hair. At Melanie's request, he was growing it a little longer than his typical crew cut, and he wasn't used to how it felt. "After a day like today, I'm certainly ready for retirement," Guy responded.

Stanley could see that Guy had had a rough day. "You feel like talking about it?" he asked. He motioned toward the dining set, and the two men sat down on the antique chairs right there in the driveway. Guy told Stanley all about MegaMart and the working group.

"You warned me about how bad it is if one person won't buy into the process," Guy said. "I'm dealing with that to some extent on the Argosy team. But the whole MegaMart team is uncooperative. The leader of the team won't lead. I've tried to set an example of accountability, but beyond that, I'm out of tricks. I have no idea how to make the MegaMart members act more accountable to the rest of the working group."

Stanley pondered this for a moment as he zipped up his jacket. "You want to hear more about the *Constellation*?" he asked. "I don't want to bore you."

Guy laughed. "Your stories are never boring, Stanley," he said. "And even if they were, I'm willing to be bored if I thought I could learn something."

Stanley cleared his throat and began. "Accountability was my biggest worry when I started out on the *Constellation*," he said. "I wondered how I could possibly keep after all these people in all these different trades. It didn't seem possible. I couldn't direct them, I didn't control their paychecks, and I wasn't an expert in any of their skills. I felt like I could never be sure how well someone understood what he was accountable for."

Guy crossed his arms and nodded. "That's where I am now with the MegaMart people."

Stanley glanced sideways at Guy. "And let me guess: The schedule is starting to slip."

Guy nodded again. "How'd you know?"

"That's when I started learning, when the first deadlines fell through. Then I found out pretty fast that it didn't matter who I thought was accountable or what I thought of that person. Even if I could see exactly what went wrong and I could assign the blame perfectly, it didn't matter. At the end of each day, every single problem on that job was still mine to solve."

Guy thought back to his first talk with Stanley about the *Constellation*. "You told me how you'd bring everyone in and get the problems solved," he said. "That's the part that's not working for me. We're getting together, but I can't get the MegaMart people to address the issues."

Stanley exhaled, his breath visible in the chilly air. "Maybe I made that part sound too easy," he said.

If he'd been talking to anyone else, Guy would have said the other man sounded sheepish.

"Remember that story I told you about the master shipbuilder who was cursing me out because some design specifications were wrong?" Stanley asked. "When I got him together with the design engineer, they would not stop blaming each other. They were both being such jackasses that nothing was getting done. So I said to them both, 'I'll tell you exactly who is accountable for this screw-up. Me. I'm accountable because this is my ship. So let's all concentrate on helping me fix our problem.'" He smiled. "And they calmed down. And we fixed it."

"That's a great story," replied Guy, trying to picture himself having the same conversation with Robert and Margaret.

"The more often I did that, the more effective I became," Stanley elaborated. "It wasn't long before I started seeing everything in reverse. My first step toward solving every problem was to hold myself accountable, for *everything* that went wrong." He tapped the antique table beside him for emphasis with each word he said next. "Every single little thing."

Guy kept listening, still testing the idea in his mind.

"With every mix-up, every delay," Stanley continued, "I asked myself how I let this happen. Asking myself that question always gave me the most direct route to the solution, even if it wasn't always a comfortable process."

Guy ran a hand through his hair again. "Maybe my situation is a little different, though," he said. "MegaMart's got a lot of power and they can walk away from this working group at any minute. What do I do about people who don't care, who may be willing to sabotage the job?" His expression darkened. "Because I'm beginning to suspect that's what's going on with MegaMart."

"In general, that's a dangerous way for a leader to think," Stanley warned. "There are exceptions, but it's almost always untrue that when someone acts careless, heedless, or whatever, it's because there's something wrong with him or her."

Stanley leaned forward and rested his forearms on his knees, his hands hanging down toward the pavement. "For example, on that design screw-up, the design engineer was to blame for some shoddy drawings, no doubt about it. But he'd been doing those designs fast and on-the-fly for years, and the shipbuilders always made on-site adjustments to fix his mistakes. It wasn't until I brought the engineer and the shipbuilder together that the engineer even understood the impact his sloppy work was having on everyone else."

"So what do you think I need to do with Robert and his team?" Guy asked. He could see Stanley's point, but he wasn't sure how to apply it to the wave-and-pay work group.

"You've got to resist buying into the fallacy that Robert might be flawed in some way," Stanley said without hesitating. "Once you decide that there's something wrong with a person, all you notice about that person is the evidence that you're right, and that gets you nowhere."

Stanley sat up straight again and continued. "Instead, try assuming the best about Robert and his team. Then you'll start seeing the best in their abilities, and that's the path toward building a productive relationship. The next time they fail to meet your expectations, and I suspect they will, try to assume that they did their best. Assume that the failure was somehow your own responsibility." He smiled at Guy to soften his words.

"Do that and you won't feel victimized and let down. You will take control of your outcomes instead. You'll start accomplishing much more through the work of others, and that is what accountability is all about."

"I'm sure you're right, Stanley, but I don't know where to start," Guy said, scuffing his foot back and forth over the asphalt as he thought out loud. "Do I have to wait until Robert takes me by surprise or comes up short again?"

"The best way to start is to go in tomorrow and ask a lot of questions," Stanley replied. "Too many people take leadership jobs thinking they need to know the answers. But leadership is about knowing the right questions to ask."

"And I assume you don't mean questions like 'How could you make such a dumb mistake?'" Guy joked.

"That's right," Stanley said with a laugh. "It's all in the way you ask the questions. You don't want to be a test proctor or an interrogator. You want them to know that your questions are meant to support them."

Stanley turned in his chair so that he was facing Guy. "For instance, whenever I ask you about your work, Guy, you feel free to tell me what's on your mind because you know that I'm interested in supporting you and offering you help. That's how you want to make your team members feel when you ask questions." He chuckled. "Even if you've got a little voice inside your head screaming at them, 'How could you be so dumb?'"

"I think I'm pretty good at that already," Guy responded. It was important to him that he not fly off the handle with his subordinates or insult them. "I don't always know how to handle the answers, though."

"If you get an answer but you're still unsatisfied, then you haven't asked the right question yet," Stanley pointed out with a grin. "You have to persist with the questions, and that's where most people drop the ball. It takes moral courage to keep asking questions until you understand the situation fully."

He paused and narrowed his eyes in thought. "I'll bet there are some questions you'd like to ask Robert but haven't."

"You've read my mind again, Stanley," Guy replied. "Say, have you ever thought about getting a job as a psychic at the fair?"

"No—I think becoming an antiques dealer might be a more lucrative second career!" Stanley chuckled. He stood up, and Guy followed suit.

"In all seriousness, though, that's the challenge," Stanley said. "You're afraid to ask Robert those questions because you're afraid of how he may react, what he may think, what he might do. But that's the moral courage required by leadership. It's your job to address conflict, including any conflict stirred up by the questions you ask. You'll find that people won't be offended by your questions once you've made it clear that you're not out to blame them, that you've taken responsibility, that you want to support them."

"So what's the next question I should have for Robert?" Guy asked.

"It could be, 'How do you think this is going?'" Stanley said.

Guy responded with a laugh. He thought he could answer that one himself.

"I'm serious," Stanley continued. "A question like that could lead to the kind of conversation that you and he probably need to have."

Guy had a hard time imagining that conversation. But he promised Stanley that he would keep thinking about it.

"Now come on," Stanley exclaimed, hefting the chair on which he had been sitting. "Let's get this furniture into the garage before we freeze to death!"

CHAPTER 12

A MegaMart Monkey Wrench

Several days after the week two meeting, Ted called to ask Guy to come to his office.

Probably wants an update, Guy thought, *and to see if I have taken his team-building advice to heart.* He was surprised to find Ted at the head of a table full of unfamiliar people when he arrived at the Argosy building.

"Hold on a moment everyone," Ted told them. "I'll be right back."

Ted fixed his gaze on Guy as they moved into the reception area outside his office. "Another project," Ted explained. "I'll tell you about it when you're done with this one."

"You look busy," Guy observed. "Do you need a quick update on wave-and-pay? I can boil it down to a few sentences."

"No," Ted said, shaking his head. "I've got an update for you. MegaMart is very, very…"

He paused, making Guy's stomach flip-flop. *Very what? Angry? Disappointed? Disgusted? Distrustful?*

"…happy!" Ted finished, a smile playing at the corners of his lips. "They like where your wave-and-pay group is headed. I'm told this comes from way up near the top."

Guy could hardly believe his ears. In fact, he was fairly sure his mouth had gaped open for a split second before he remembered to close it. Based on the way Robert had handled the week two meeting, he wouldn't have been surprised if MegaMart was ready to pull out.

"It sounds like your buddy Robert is sending only good news up the line," Ted commented. "They've heard that Nigel's expertise is impressive and so is your leadership. They think it's all going very well."

"That's…nice…to hear," Guy said, weighing his words. He wondered if perhaps there was a method behind Robert's strange way of doing things. Maybe Robert was a good fit for MegaMart's strange corporate culture.

"Now here's what you need to know," Ted said, sitting down on a nearby sofa. "They are *so* happy at MegaMart that they want to raise their level of commitment. They're ready to make a serious investment in their store systems. They were tentative about this before. Now they're not. So that's really good news."

"That's *great* news," Guy replied, taking a chair opposite Ted. "Because so far, they've been withholding their per-store budget, which has made it almost impossible to narrow down our choices."

"I've got the answer for you," Ted announced.

Guy's eyebrows rose. *Really? Well, that was easy... I think.*

"They're ready to move forward on Shopper Xpress," said Ted. "It's official. You will need to include Shopper Xpress as the ultimate goal of the group mission."

"I'd love to," said Guy. He held up a hand. "But what's Shopper Xpress?"

Ted looked surprised. "My MegaMart contact told me you would know what that was," he replied. "He was certain Robert had told you all about it."

Guy shook his head. *I knew this sudden cooperation was too good to be true!*

"I have only a few minutes before I need to get back to my meeting, but let me tell you what I know," Ted said.

He explained that Shopper Xpress was MegaMart's concept for the speedy self-checkout store of the future. Every MegaMart store item would carry a hidden radio-sensitive chip inside its price tag. When a shopper passes through the checkout area, all the contents of the shopper's cart would be scanned electronically and added up instantaneously. There would be no need to remove each item from the cart and scan it individually. Then the phone in the shopper's pocket or purse would also be scanned and billed.

"It would work seamlessly, like an automated tollbooth on the turnpike," Ted finished. "Only it would bill your account for your socks, your toothpaste, and your breakfast cereal, instead of your car."

Pensive, Guy remained silent and studied the tops of his shoes. The toe of his right loafer needed a little polish, he saw.

"What?" Ted asked. "What's the problem?"

Guy looked up. "Nothing like this has ever come up at our meetings," he admitted. "Never. Our charge was to discuss existing technologies, and this sounds completely new. I don't know if it's compatible with CellMobile's phones or with anything else we've studied so far. I don't know if we—" He stopped, thinking back to his conversation on accountability with Stanley. "I don't know if *I* can deliver this."

"Well, we've got to deliver it," Ted said, putting on what Guy thought of as his "Big Boss" expression. "It's what MegaMart wants. I don't need to explain that again. We're playing a game of heads they win, tails we lose."

Again, Guy was baffled. "What do you mean by that?"

"It means that we all win if your group succeeds," Ted explained. "But if your group can't deliver, then the only loser is Argosy. MegaMart is fine either way. So is CellMobile. If we can't bring this home, MegaMart and CellMobile can afford to learn from our failure and find a different partner to make a gazillion dollars with. Then we'll be on the outside looking in while another firm takes what should have been ours."

The knot of anxiety in Guy's gut suddenly seemed twice as big.

Ted rose, gave Guy a pat on the shoulder, and started back toward his meeting. "I gotta go," he said. "Make it work. I have confidence in you."

Guy was lost in thought as he stood and headed toward the elevators. At first, he didn't notice Mike Andrews emerge through one of the doors.

"Are you okay, Guy?" Mike asked, causing Guy's attention to snap back to reality. "You don't look so good."

"I don't?" Guy asked. He couldn't believe his emotions were so transparent. He thought he had developed a pretty good poker face over the years.

"What's wrong?" Mike looked concerned.

"It's MegaMart," Guy began. It pained him to confirm Mike's suspicions about the company. "They've added something new to the working group's mission. I don't think we can pull it off. I won't bore you with the details." He finished with a sigh.

"Try not to take it too hard," Mike replied. His voice was tinged with sympathy. "This is MegaMart's way. Every time you solve a problem for them, it costs them nothing to toss you another, and then another."

Mike was making sense, as much as Guy hated to admit it.

"You watch," Mike went on. "When your group is finished with its report, MegaMart will say thank you very much, and then they'll cut Argosy and CellMobile loose." He paused and rolled his eyes. "On second thought, they probably won't even say thank you."

"I wish you were participating more in the working group," Guy commented. "This kind of thinking might keep us on our toes."

"You're not listening," Mike said. His sympathetic tone had evaporated. "You're the captain of the Titanic here, Guy. Let it sink and find a lifeboat. The best thing for all of us would be for this working group to collapse before this next meeting. Then you and everyone else can go back to work, making real money with real clients."

Guy thought for a moment as Mike studied his reaction. "You're right, Mike," he concluded. "These meetings are a waste of your time. Why don't you skip the rest of them?"

"I was planning to anyway," Mike said with a smirk. "But thank you for the invitation." He started to walk away.

"But do me this favor," Guy continued, stopping Mike in his tracks. "Send Freddie from your office, instead. He's got a real passion for mobile marketing, and he's learning a lot from Nigel. I'll ask Freddie to pester the MegaMart people for details. That way, who knows? We might get something out of this before it comes apart."

"Now you're talking sensibly," Mike pronounced. He seemed proud to hear Guy strike a note of cynicism. "But leave me on the list, and for goodness' sake, don't tell Ted I'm not coming to meetings anymore. Make *sure* I'm still on that list."

Guy nodded. "Will do. See you around, Mike."

When Guy returned to his office, he called Nigel and Freddie and asked them to meet him in the café downstairs to talk strategy on Shopper Xpress. The week four meeting was a little more than a week away, and MegaMart's big last-minute change had thrown a monkey wrench into a plan that was already on shaky ground.

"I'm wondering if I should have seen this coming," Nigel said after the three men had settled in their seats.

Unless Guy's eyes were deceiving him, Nigel's bowtie of the day was actually adorned with miniature beagles. He shook his head and redirected his attention to what the other man was saying.

"I knew that MegaMart's biggest headache is its checkout lines," Nigel confirmed. "The company keeps prices low by understaffing its registers and installing self-checkout stations, but shoppers get frustrated by the long lines. It's the number-one reason consumers avoid MegaMart. Shopper Xpress would be the perfect solution."

"Really?" Guy asked. It seemed incredible that this one system could solve the retail giant's biggest problem.

"It's perfect," Nigel replied. "Or it would be, if it could be done. But it can't. The technology isn't ready. There's one experimental 'contactless shopping' store in Germany that has tried something like this, and the result has been an absolute mess."

"What's the problem?" Freddie asked. "Is it really that complicated?"

Freddie's face displayed genuine curiosity. *I was right to bring him on board*, Guy thought.

"One problem is that it all works *too well*," Nigel explained. "You walk into this store in downtown Hamburg, fill your cart, and all the products have these little pricing chips hidden inside them. Then you go through the checkout area."

Guy and Freddie nodded in unison.

"But say you've got a pen in your pocket that you bought yesterday," Nigel continued. "The scanner charges you for it again. It will charge you for the shoes on your feet, the hat on your head, everything that's got these pricing chips hidden in them. So you have to stop and hold up the line and have a cashier go over all the items you're legitimately buying, which defeats the entire purpose of the system."

"That's crazy!" Freddie exclaimed.

"They're trying to make some fixes," Nigel added. "But everyone in the industry assumes that they are years away from going mainstream with it."

"Nigel, when was the last time you visited a MegaMart?" Guy asked.

Nigel admitted that he'd never been in one. "All the stores are in the suburbs, and I rarely rent a car when I visit the U.S."

Guy handed Freddie his car keys. "I want you two to do me a big favor," he said. "Find one of the newer MegaMarts, go in, and see what you can find. Take notes on how they operate."

"You want us to just wander around?" Freddie asked, jingling the keys in his palm. "What are we looking for?"

"We'll know it when we see it," Nigel answered, looking excited. "It's a good idea."

Guy reached in his pocket and took out a shopping list Melanie had given him the day before. Then he opened his wallet and pulled out a few twenty dollar bills. "Pick up these items for me," he instructed, handing the cash and list to Freddie. "As you're shopping, take some notes on the displays, the physical space, what you think it might take for MegaMart to make this kind of change."

"What about next Friday's meeting?" Nigel asked as they all stood up. "Do you want me to be ready to talk about Shopper Xpress?"

"I don't think so," Guy replied. "But if Friday goes badly, I'm sure we'll need to prepare something about it before week six."

"Speaking of Friday," Nigel said. "Have you told Margaret at CellMobile about this?"

"No." Guy winced at the thought. "Not yet."

"Good luck, mate," Nigel told him. He gave Guy his crooked grin. "Because she is going to freak out."

Believe me, I know, Guy thought. Aloud he said, "You two have fun running that errand! My wife says thanks." He winked and headed back upstairs to tackle his never-ending to-do list... and to worry some more.

PART THREE

CHAPTER 13

No Good Deed Goes Unpunished

The suburbs of New Jersey whizzed past the Acela train window as Guy sipped at his coffee. He was paging through a trade magazine article Nigel had found about the experimental German store. The title of the article was "Haywire in Hamburg."

Right out of the gate, the system doesn't seem very promising, Guy reflected.

His thoughts drifted back to the previous day. After he'd sent Nigel and Freddie on their shopping errand, Guy had called Margaret and asked if he could visit her at the CellMobile offices in Manhattan. "I've got a few things I need to go over with you in person," he'd said.

"That sounds a little ominous," Margaret replied.

He promised her it was nothing they couldn't handle. But now, as Guy looked over all the mishaps that befell shoppers in the Hamburg experimental store, he wasn't so sure.

The CellMobile building in midtown was a soaring granite edifice with a large, inviting shopping mall occupying its bottom three levels. After Guy rode the elevator to Margaret's upper floor, he found her waiting in the lobby area as he stepped off. She led him to her office.

"I'm ready," she announced, placing her palms flat on her desk in an exaggerated gesture. "I've braced myself. What's the news?"

"The news is that MegaMart wants this thing they call Shopper Xpress," said Guy. He handed her a copy of some of Nigel's documentation from the Hamburg store, but he kept the "Haywire in Hamburg" story to himself. "It's a system for automatically ringing up every item in the shopping cart instead of scanning them one-by-one."

"This looks great," murmured Margaret, as she flipped through the documents. "But what's this got to do with wave-and-pay?"

"Here's the part you might not like so much," Guy told her. "MegaMart wants this system to be completely hands-off. They want to give shoppers a seamless experience, so that they don't even need to remove their phones from their pockets or purses."

"So I would just walk through the checkout?" Margaret asked, trying to understand. "And, bingo, like I was in some space-age movie, my items would be rung up, my phone would be billed, and that's it?"

"That's what they want," confirmed Guy. He hoped that maybe Margaret wouldn't be a tough sell after all.

His hopes were dashed as an expression of unmistakable annoyance crept onto her face. She looked at the documentation again. "How do all the items get bagged up?" she asked. "What about customers who might want to double-check their totals before committing to buying everything in their carts? And where do you get your receipt? This idea seems a little half-baked."

"I don't think they've thought it through," Guy explained. "But they are obsessed with reducing the waiting time in their checkout lines. They assume this will run as smoothly as an automated toll system, like E-ZPass, or SunPass in Florida."

Margaret rolled her eyes and muttered something that didn't sound complimentary under her breath. "It's not that simple with cell phones as the payment medium," she said in a louder voice. "The first issue is security. Every wave-and-pay system requires a shopper to punch in a four-digit PIN-code number. That confirms that the phone hasn't been stolen or borrowed."

Guy took notes. He didn't interrupt.

Margaret went on, sounding like a displeased teacher correcting a pupil who had gotten an answer all wrong. "Second, wave-and-pay requires waving the phone within four inches of the point-of-sale sensor. That's also for security. If your phone data were readable at any greater distance, then a hacker with a portable scanner could raid your account as you walk down the street. But even if you wanted to read our phone chips from three or four feet away, that would require such a high signal strength that it would violate federal communications law. Does MegaMart want to change the law?" She threw up her hands.

"I hadn't thought of that," Guy responded. Actually, he hadn't *known* any of that.

"MegaMart is the one that should be thinking of it," Margaret retorted. "They've got a lot of work to do if they want to pull this off."

Guy looked at her, knowing that she *really* wouldn't like what he had to say next. "It's our work to do," he said. "MegaMart has moved the goalposts. My boss, Ted, says that this is MegaMart's new baseline standard for a successful mobile payment system. By week four, MegaMart wants each of our three alternative systems to be compatible with Shopper Xpress."

"How can they do this?" Margaret asked, almost shouting. Her temper was rising. "How can they throw a problem this big in our laps and expect us to solve it?"

"This is what they do," Guy said, reaching up to run a hand through his hair. He certainly understood Margaret's frustration. "Ted told me they were so encouraged by our initial progress that they decided to up the ante. They're reaching for a system they had assumed was years away."

"No good deed goes unpunished with them," Margaret snapped. She looked out the window as a news helicopter glided by. "It's only been five weeks and I'm already fed up with Robert and that crew of his." Her gaze returned to Guy. "Have you tried to get through to Frank and Vera during the week? Everything is a one-way street. Information goes into MegaMart, but it doesn't come out."

"I've got to do a better job with them, I know," he conceded.

"*You're* fine," Margaret corrected him. "This is on *them*."

Guy nodded. "Yes, it's true that MegaMart is causing a mess," he said. "But I'm the leader, which means I'm also the cleanup crew, and I need your help. Can you, or someone on your staff, write a memo about what you've told me?"

He thought for a second. "Give me as much detail as you can about the security and signal-strength problems with Shopper Xpress. Put in whatever potential solutions you can think of, too. If you get the memo to me before the end of the day today, I'll get Nigel's take on it, merge the documents under my name and send it to Robert tonight."

Margaret agreed to draft the memo, still grumbling about the situation. "Robert is the real problem here, you know," she pointed out. "You were the first to notice how he has no clout with his team. He doesn't seem to be able to tell his bosses any bad news, either. He's in the wrong job, and we're all paying the price."

"Personally, I'm finished blaming Robert," Guy said.

Margaret's eyebrows shot upward.

"I am," Guy confirmed. "I'm going to assume we need him to succeed in order for us all to succeed. My hope is that this memo will help him out. If we give him a specific list of items to work with, maybe he can get his team to think creatively and stretch for some solutions. He says he likes the SMART process, so I'll try to frame it in SMART goal terms. "

"That's ironic," Margaret muttered, "because so much of what I've learned about that company is so dumb."

Guy resisted the temptation to indulge Margaret's anger. He changed the subject and the two spent another 20 minutes talking about CellMobile's plans for new smartphones. Then Guy excused himself to catch a train home.

During the Acela ride to Philadelphia, Guy called Nigel. "Did you enjoy shopping for my groceries?" he asked.

"Except for the cheese. Is it supposed to smell that bad?" Nigel asked. "Because I think I can still smell it on my jacket."

"Sorry about that," Guy chuckled. "What about the store? Did you see anything interesting?"

"The wait for checkout is a definite problem," Nigel confirmed. "The lines were six or seven deep. But we noticed that a big part of the delay is putting all the purchased items in bags. Freddie and I agreed that Shopper Xpress would require a big store redesign. They need to add an open bagging area for shoppers after they go through Shopper Xpress. Otherwise the wait in line won't change that much. There were a few other things we noticed, too."

"Could you write up your thoughts in a memo before you go home today?" Guy asked as he watched the landscape blur by. "I'll combine it with what Margaret's told me and give Robert's team a chance to help solve the problems we see."

Nigel agreed, and couldn't resist making another comment about the cheese before hanging up. Then Guy made another call. This one was to Melanie.

"My train is getting in a little after six," he told her. "Do you think you could find a sitter for the girls and meet me downtown for dinner?"

"Sure," said Melanie, sounding surprised. "What's the occasion?"

"The occasion is that I'm not working late tonight," Guy exclaimed. "Everywhere I look, I've managed to put the ball in someone else's court. I don't know how I did it, but I've got nothing left to do. It feels a little strange!"

Chapter 14

Clarity and Courage

As he ate his chicken Caesar salad that night, Guy told Melanie about his meeting with Margaret earlier in the day.

"Stanley says I have to assume everything that goes wrong is my responsibility," he said in between bites. "So I'm trying that out, trying to steer clear of assigning blame and look only at my own responsibility to fix this whole mess."

Melanie scowled. "That seems harsh," she responded, twirling some linguine onto her fork. "How can you take responsibility just because MegaMart is asking for the moon? They sound crazy at that company. How can that be your fault?"

"It's not a matter of fault," Guy responded. He speared a piece of chicken. "That's what Stanley helped me see. I didn't obsess today over what was wrong with Robert. That gave me some clarity in deciding what I need to do to set things right."

He looked up at Melanie. "That chat with him was really helpful. I'm not sure today would have been the same if I hadn't talked to him last week."

Melanie laughed. "Then I'm glad I got him outside to help me with that dining room set! You might not have asked him for his advice otherwise."

Melanie's mention of the dining room set reminded Guy that he'd been going on about work for too long. "I told Stanley how amazingly well your antique business is going," he shared. "He's very impressed with you. I am, too."

Melanie's face broke out into a pleased smile. "It's so funny to think about it," she reflected. "When I was growing up, I really didn't like working at my parents' shop. I wanted to get out on the beach every day and away from all those smelly old antiques. And now, look at me!"

"Do the antiques smell any better these days?" Guy asked, taking a sip of his wine.

"Now they smell like money," she said with a laugh. "Seriously, the antique smells sometimes remind me of my parents. Now that they're both gone, it's a nice feeling. It's a connection."

Melanie went on to tell Guy about her day, which hadn't gone very well. She saw some antiques she liked a lot, she said, but had been unable to get her price. After a long day of bargain hunting, she had come up empty.

"Some of my friends have teased me that I've discovered a way to get paid to go shopping every day, but I'm not sure they're really kidding," Melanie complained. She tore off a piece of her garlic bread. "The truth is that this is nothing like shopping. With shopping, you get to buy what you like. This is a business. If I ask for my price and if I can't get it, then I'm not buying. That's what happened today, over and over again. It was so frustrating." She popped the bread into her mouth.

"Is it possible you're not offering to pay enough?" Guy asked.

"No," she replied. "That's the discipline in negotiating. Ask for a low-to-reasonable price and then walk away if they won't meet it. On the sell side, I start by asking high and then I stick to my minimum, or I walk. A lot of people in this business compromise too easily on price. They're afraid to stick by the price they ask for."

Guy thought about that for a moment, listening to the low hum of conversation in the restaurant. "It's interesting, because Stanley says that asking requires moral courage," he told Melanie. "I hadn't thought of it before, but it's true. It takes courage to ask for what you want and not let the other party talk you out of it."

Melanie nodded. "My mother taught me how to negotiate," she said. "She always told me that if you make a low offer that's not insulting, most people are afraid to ask for more. And if you're selling, and you act confident about your high asking price, most people will be afraid to ask you to lower it."

She paused while their waitress refilled her water glass. "That's the whole difference between making money in antiques and barely getting by. The secret is to be less afraid to ask than the other guy. I guess that's what Stanley would call courage."

"To courage!" said Guy, and he lifted his wine glass as Melanie lifted hers.

"To Stanley!" she responded.

When Guy and Melanie got home, Melanie went in to check on the girls while Guy got out his laptop and opened his email. As promised, Margaret and Nigel had both sent him their assessments of Shopper Xpress. He took about 20 minutes going over the two documents, and then spent another half hour merging their two lists of concerns into one memo.

At the top of the memo, Guy wrote a personal note to Robert: "Please give your team members copies of this memo so we can all begin to think collaboratively about overcoming these obstacles to Shopper Xpress. Looking forward to the discussion!"

Guy hit "send" and then headed off to bed. He slept soundly that night, more soundly than he had in weeks.

CHAPTER 15

Impasse

Taylor sat on the edge of the chair in Guy's office. Every so often, she brought her index finger up to her mouth as though to bite her nail, then jerked her hand back into her lap. Guy was reading her social media plan for Flavor Burst, and the effort seemed very thin and unimaginative. He felt she was being entirely too cautious.

"Does this look like it will be enough, Taylor?" he asked.

"I know there's not a lot on the page," she said, not quite meeting his eyes. "I was hoping we could talk about some ideas here."

Guy handed the document back to her. "Here's what I'd like you to do," he instructed. "Get your team together and come back to me with 20 more of these kinds of items. Do you know Freddie in Mike Andrews' office? Run it by him, too. Between Freddie and your team, I'll bet you can come up with 30."

Taylor looked a little stunned at the assignment. She thanked Guy, calling him "Mr. Cedrick," and left. Only a few seconds later, Linda appeared in the doorway.

"Flavor Burst's social media plan needs a lot of work," Guy pointed out.

"You're reaping what you've sown," she stated, unrepentant. "You've micromanaged for so long that some people have gotten a little lazy. You help them when you should be challenging them. If they don't stretch creatively, it's because they're used to you telling them what to do."

"Taylor's got her challenge now," Guy responded, leaning back in his chair and interlocking his fingers behind his head. "I told her to add 30 items to that social media plan."

"Keep that up, Boss," Linda suggested. "The word will get around."

Guy looked at the clock. The week four meeting was an hour away. "Speaking of challenges," he said, "I've got to get going."

"That was a great memo you sent to Robert," Linda commented as Guy gathered the materials he needed and put them in his briefcase. "What did he make of it?"

"I've heard nothing from him, as usual," Guy muttered. He grabbed his overcoat. "But we'll know the answer soon."

Guy opened the week four meeting with a presentation that closely reflected the contents of his memo to Robert. As he ticked off the potential obstacles to Shopper Xpress, he noticed that Frank and Vera were looking confused and whispering to each other.

Finally, Frank interrupted Guy just as he was about to wrap up the presentation. "This is the first time I'm seeing this," he said, his frustration leaking into voice. "Where did this list of obstacles come from?"

Guy evaded the question and patiently focused on finishing the last segment of his presentation. Then, after suggesting that the group take a five-minute break, he motioned Robert to follow him outside the conference room.

"We've got to stop meeting like this," Robert joked.

Guy didn't laugh.

"Why would Frank ask me that?" Guy wondered, cutting to the chase. "Didn't you give him the memo?"

"Yeah, I know. I'm sorry. But I couldn't share that with Frank and Vera," Robert explained.

Guy didn't try to keep the look of incredulity from his face. "I sent that memo so that they *would* see it," he stated.

"That wasn't something I wanted circulating in our building prior to this meeting." Robert shifted his feet. "It suggested that Shopper Xpress might not work, and I was afraid if the wrong person saw it, our team might get pulled from the group."

"But if you don't share these kinds of obstacles with your tech team, how are we supposed to overcome them?" Guy tried to hide his exasperation. "Help me understand what you're thinking."

"I had to use my better judgment," Robert explained. "I can't risk allowing certain people above me to think that I'm undermining them." He pointed toward the ceiling. "Someone high up—and I don't know who—really wants Shopper Xpress. MegaMart is ready to spend big on outfitting the stores for it."

Robert glanced back toward the conference room and seemed to become more confident. "Now we think it's up to CellMobile to resolve any issues with the cell phone interface so we can move forward."

"But CellMobile says that the system your bosses want isn't practical or possible," Guy replied. "One crucial piece violates the law. Can't you tell them that? There's a clear need for them to revise their project requirements."

Robert frowned and scuffed one of his shoes against the carpet. "Can you be sure that CellMobile is making serious attempts to tackle those issues?" he asked. "What if they're not up to the task? What if there's another cell phone provider that is? Those are the questions my bosses will ask me. What should I tell them?"

Guy realized in that moment that Robert would never take the risks necessary to make the working group succeed. From Robert's perspective, blaming the group's failure on CellMobile was much more preferable than asking his superiors to compromise their vision for Shopper Xpress.

I'm going to have to think of a different way to handle this, Guy told himself. *But how?*

When Guy and Robert returned to the conference room, Margaret and her team were standing at the door. Guy had a feeling that it wasn't a good sign. He was right.

Margaret waited until Robert and Guy were inside before she spoke. "We've had enough," she said. "It's been nice working with you, but we're not getting back on the train in two weeks only to be subjected to this kind of treatment all over again."

"You're not quitting, are you?" The thought terrified Guy.

"No, we can't quit," Margaret replied.

Guy felt himself start to breathe again.

"But we're stepping back," Margaret continued. "We've given you tons of information, more than enough for you to get to the next step on your own. Let us know when your team and Robert's team have gotten past this Shopper Xpress fantasy. We'll rejoin you when you've produced the three alternative wave-and-pay systems that we were originally scheduled to discuss today."

"I can't promise you that I can do that," Guy told her.

Margaret ignored him. "We will come to the week six meeting if we receive the specs for those three alternative systems within the next week," she announced. "But if MegaMart still won't budge off Shopper Xpress, then we all need to acknowledge that we've come to an impasse, don't you think?"

Guy didn't know how to respond, so he motioned everyone back to the conference table. He led the rest of the meeting in a fog. The CellMobile team said little, although Margaret and the other members responded pleasantly to questions about phone specifications.

Nigel and Vera from MegaMart monopolized most of the remaining time by debating various details of wireless in-store marketing and electronic coupons—safe areas to discuss since neither were reliant on Shopper Xpress.

Nigel had made some copies of the article "Haywire in Hamburg." They sat in a pile in the middle of the table, untouched.

Chapter 16

Where the Buck *Really* Stops

After lunch, Nigel, Freddie, Linda, and Guy sat in Eaton/Argosy's empty conference room, mulling over what had gone wrong that day.

"I've never seen anything like that before," said a morose Nigel. "I'd heard stories about MegaMart, but I had no idea they operated like this."

Linda gave a rueful laugh. "I've seen it before," she commented. "This feels a lot like the TrekPhone campaign we did with them."

Guy had to agree. The TrekPhone project had certainly been full of miscommunications and differing expectations.

"I kind of feel bad for Robert," Freddie put in.

Nigel stared at him like he had grown a second head. "How can you say that?" he asked, his tone dripping incredulity.

"I think Robert has lousy bosses," Freddie explained. He tapped himself on the chest. "I compare myself to him, and I feel lucky. I've got Mike, who put me on this great team. I've got you three, and you've all got Ted. You're all people I know I can get help from, or talk with, like this."

Freddie shrugged. "Who has Robert got? I don't think he's got anyone."

The four were silent for a moment, and then Nigel spoke up. "Freddie, show Guy what you drew up earlier today."

Freddie pulled out a sketchpad with some scribbled diagrams on it. "I thought of this after Nigel and I went out to that MegaMart," he said. "I had to buy a pound of smoked sliced turkey for Guy—"

"For Melanie, really," Guy interjected with a laugh.

"Yeah, for *Melanie*," Freddie continued. "So I went to the deli counter, took a little paper number from the dispenser, and waited in line. And that's when it hit me."

"What hit you?" Guy had no idea what Freddie was talking about.

"They control the lines at the deli by having you take a number," Freddie explained. "Nothing innovative there. But it made me think, why couldn't Shopper Xpress work the same way?"

"You're not explaining this very well at all," Nigel commented. He pursed his lips and tapped his pen against the table.

"Okay. Picture this," said Freddie, taking a different approach. "You walk into MegaMart and before you do anything, you check *in* with your phone at a little kiosk with a keypad. You wave your phone and punch in your PIN code number."

"So you split up the wave-and-pay process, is that right?" Guy asked. He thought he was catching Freddie's drift now.

"You do the wave and PIN code on the way in, and then save the actual billing for when you leave?"

"Exactly. When you check in, you've authenticated your phone and confirmed your identity," Freddie explained. "Then, at the checkout counter, you don't have to slow down to wave your phone up close and re-enter your PIN code. You've already done that when you checked in. It should be no problem to have your phone recognized and billed automatically, without a PIN code, as you pass through the checkout area."

Guy thought for a moment. "That's a very creative way to address what Margaret said about security," he said, proud that a member of his team had taken such initiative. "But what about signal strength? CellMobile is certain it would require a change in the law to read the phone from three or four feet away at checkout."

"That's why I didn't ask Freddie to discuss it at the meeting," Nigel replied. "We've got no answer for that, and I didn't want to confuse the issue—though I doubt that anyone could confuse the issue worse than Robert already has." He heaved a put-upon sigh.

Guy looked out the conference room's windows without really seeing the view. As he thought about what to do next, Stanley's words about blame and accountability came to his mind.

"I think I've been approaching this the wrong way," Guy admitted to the group. "I can't keep expecting Robert to rally his team, and I can't keep expecting him to send negative news up the line. It's not his fault."

He ignored Nigel's raised eyebrows and Linda's eye-roll and continued. "I have to ask Ted if I can go over Robert's head. Someone higher up at MegaMart needs to make a choice. Either they cooperate with us and help address the problems with Shopper Xpress, or we go back to the original plan for wave-and-pay. In fact, I'm going to go call Ted now."

Ted was unavailable to meet with Guy until 4:30, which made Guy nervous. Ted was usually tired at the end of the day, and the end of the day on Friday was the worst time of the week to ask Ted for anything. But Guy decided this was one talk he couldn't put off until after the weekend. If nothing else, *he* would rest easier once it was over.

"I've already heard about your group meeting today," Ted told Guy as soon as he arrived at Argosy's main office. "What are you going to do about this?"

"Margaret thinks we're at an impasse," Guy replied. "She doesn't see CellMobile's technology working with Shopper Xpress, so she's pulling her team back. She wants Argosy and MegaMart to drop Shopper Xpress and come to an agreement on three alternative wave-and-pay systems, as we agreed to in the original plan for the working group."

Ted nodded. "So what do you want to do?"

"I'd like to go over Robert's head," Guy responded. "If you could put me in touch with his supervisor, I could explain why we're deadlocked. That way, either we'll get better cooperation from Robert's team in solving the problems with Shopper

Xpress, or those problems will finally get communicated up the MegaMart chain of command."

"That would accomplish nothing," Ted said, almost before the words were out of Guy's mouth. "Robert's boss is under the same pressure as Robert. They're both expected to make Shopper Xpress work. What else have you got?"

Guy wasn't prepared for Ted to react so abruptly. "What if you told your MegaMart contacts about the problem?" Thrown off-balance, he stammered slightly as the words came out. "Can you tell them that CellMobile thinks Shopper Xpress is fatally flawed?"

"I *could* do that," Ted agreed. "But it will probably mean the end of the working group. Because Shopper Xpress is what MegaMart wants, and MegaMart doesn't settle for less than that. Ask them to settle and they'll say, 'No thanks, we'll pass,' instead. They'll quit us and go find another partner. Is that what you want, Guy?"

"No," Guy replied, feeling embarrassed. "Of course not."

"Let's talk about Robert then," Ted replied. His posture relaxed, signaling to Guy that the chastisement was over. "What exactly is wrong with him?"

"Robert can't solve this problem," Guy explained. "This goes beyond him. The MegaMart and CellMobile teams are deadlocked. If we can't move the discussion up the chain of command at MegaMart, then I don't know what else we can do."

"That's mighty big of you, to avoid blaming Robert," Ted observed. He pointed his finger at Guy. "But are you sure you've done your best to get through to him and his team that it's their responsibility to help figure this out? If you have, then that's fine. That's all you can do."

Ted unscrewed the cap of a bottle of water on his desk. "But I've seen my share of failures over the last 30 years, Guy. The only ones that still sting are the ones where I know that I didn't do my best."

"I think I've done everything I can," Guy confirmed as Ted took a swig of his water. "Robert is poorly suited for this role at MegaMart. He seems isolated and trusts no one. He's told me as much. He has no mentor there, no one to talk to—not the way you and I are talking now."

Ted looked at Guy with surprise. "He has *you*," Ted said.

"I'm not at MegaMart," Guy replied, after a brief pause. "I'm not his boss…"

"Aren't you his leader on this project?" Ted asked. "Besides, you listen to Stanley all the time, and he's not your boss *or* your project leader. He's just a friend and neighbor."

Guy fell silent and only nodded. He had the sinking feeling that there was, in fact, a *lot* he could have done to help Robert, but hadn't.

"You've told me that you've done everything to get Robert and his team fully involved," Ted said. "Now I'm wondering if that's true."

Ted put the water bottle down and began ticking questions off on his fingers. "Have you ever asked Robert directly to do anything he doesn't want to do? Have you ever coached him through a jam, the way Stanley has done for you? The way I've done? The way I'm doing right now?"

"No," Guy replied. "I haven't."

"I've heard you call Robert the weak link in the group before," Ted observed. "Now, I'm going to say the following to you only because I know you will take it in the spirit I'm offering it." He stared at Guy without blinking. "If you don't do everything humanly possible to help him and his team succeed, then he is not the weak link in your group. You are."

Guy felt the shock of Ted's pronouncement wash over him. He looked at his watch. He wondered if he would be able to reach Robert this late in the day so that he could ask for a meeting on Monday, or even over the weekend. It was the only thing left for Guy to do.

"It sounds to me like you've got about a week to turn this project around," Ted concluded. "It may still fail, despite your best efforts. But if you don't try to do everything you can to get MegaMart and CellMobile to play nice together, it will always feel like you chose to pull the plug on this project."

Somehow, Ted managed to look even more serious than he had a few moments ago. "Because, make no mistake, it's your choice right now whether this thing lives or dies. No one else's."

CHAPTER 17

Moral Courage at Work

The following Monday, Guy made the trip to the MegaMart headquarters. He hadn't been able to reach Robert over the weekend, so he had emailed the other man to let him know that he would be coming. Embarking on the long drive was something of a risk (after all, what if Robert called in sick?), but Guy felt that it was his duty to do everything in his power to repair the situation.

The MegaMart headquarters building was located on a desolate industrial highway not far from Dulles Airport in suburban Virginia. Security at the building's entrance reminded him of a military installation. Guy had to run a gantlet of metal detectors and identification checks just to get inside.

"It's such a great surprise to see you here," Robert said as he met Guy in the lobby. He had evidently gotten Guy's email. "Let's go to the cafeteria. Are you hungry?"

The vast cafeteria had a soaring three-story ceiling and enormous windows that overlooked the local landscape of fast food restaurants and warehouses. As Guy approached his chair and began to prepare his first sentence, he wondered why it had taken him so long to follow one of Stanley's simplest pieces of advice.

After they were seated, Guy turned to his host and asked, "So, Robert, how do you think things are going?"

"Obviously, they're not going very well," Robert stammered, trying to hide his embarrassment. "You wouldn't have to come all the way down here if they were going well."

"No one expects smooth sailing on a project like this," Guy replied. "I'm just here to see if we can get your team more involved in addressing CellMobile's issues with Shopper Xpress."

Robert relaxed, his entire posture becoming less rigid. "My team tells me they need to see proposals from CellMobile before they can give any constructive input," he said, falling back on his usual response. "I have to take their word for it. I'm not their boss. I can't tell them what to do. You may not know this, but Hans and Vera are both higher up on the totem poll around here than I am." He glanced toward the high ceiling as though to illustrate just how far above him the other two team members were.

"So tell me what *you* think," Guy prompted. "Do you think CellMobile and Argosy are capable of getting to the next stage without any help from your team?"

Robert nodded, but said nothing

"Is Frank here today?" Guy asked. "And Vera?"

"Frank is on the West Coast," Robert replied, reaching into the bag of chips on his tray. "And Vera, as you know, works on the wireless mobile marketing piece with Nigel. She doesn't know anything about payment systems like Shopper Xpress."

"How about Hans?" Guy went on. "Now that I'm here, do you think I can meet him? Would you mind calling him to see if he can come down and talk to us for a few minutes?"

"Gee, at the last minute?" Robert looked nervous. He chewed and swallowed a handful of barbeque chips before continuing. "He's the top retail technologist we have and he's awfully busy. I don't know if he'd appreciate being bothered like this."

Guy had expected an answer like this one, and thanks to Stanley, he knew what his strategy was going to be. "I know, but it's been months now and I really need to meet him." He shifted in his chair as he got ready for the speech he'd prepared. "Robert, I want to share a little coaching I received from a friend of mine named Stanley who once led the overhaul of an 80,000-ton aircraft carrier. He told me that asking questions, and asking people to do things for you, sometimes requires moral courage. That's where we are right now, you and me."

Robert was frowning, but he hadn't interrupted. Guy took a sip of his iced tea and went on.

"I'm doing my best to deliver these three alternative Shopper Xpress projects by week six. But I don't think I have a chance of succeeding unless we get Hans involved, and Vera, too. So I'm asking you to do something that maybe you would rather not do. I'm asking you to get us all together today. You, me, Hans, and Vera. Any time today. I'm willing to wait."

Robert was silent for a moment. Then he nodded, excused himself, and walked over into a corner with his phone. He made one brief call, and then another. On the second, he visibly shrugged and held up his hands a few times. That, Guy assumed, was Robert's call to Hans. But within the next hour, both Hans and Vera had appeared in the cafeteria.

Guy began by asking Hans, a lanky man who appeared to be in his forties, his opinion of Shopper Xpress. Hans did little to hide his lack of enthusiasm. He was convinced that the technology wasn't ready. He ticked off the same three concerns about security and signal strength that Margaret had offered in her memo two weeks earlier. He also mentioned a whole host of practical reasons why it would be hard to ensure that the Shopper Xpress scanner could read every item in the store.

After hearing Hans out, Guy reached into his briefcase and pulled out Freddie's sketch of a proposal for cell phone check-in kiosks. "Before we write this thing off, take a look at what one of my team members came up with," he suggested.

Hans studied Freddie's drawings for about a minute.

"This is an interesting approach," Hans said, propping his elbow on the table cradling his chin in his palm. "It takes care of everything except that signal-strength problem at checkout." He pondered the sheet for a moment longer and then turned to Vera. "For the wireless network," he asked her, "are you planning to install a storewide mesh network or go with ad-hoc Wi-Fi?"

Vera's response was beyond Guy's comprehension. For three full minutes, Robert, Hans, and Vera chattered in dense technical terminology, with growing animation. Guy stayed silent and hoped that their lively discussion was a good sign.

Finally Hans said, "That should work. Why wouldn't that work?"

Guy smiled. It was time for a translation. "Dumb it down for me, Robert," he said. "Pretend I'm ten years old."

Robert began to explain. "Once a shopper checks in at the kiosk with a cell phone and a PIN-code number, the cell phone connects to the store's mobile marketing wireless mesh network. That's the Wi-Fi network that tracks your phone in the store and sends you electronic coupons. As long as your phone has been authenticated, the same network can also handle wireless billing at checkout. Normally, we'd never dream of billing through the mesh network because it's not secure enough. But the check-in process makes it secure."

Hans was a little more cautious. "I can't say how smooth the handoffs would be," he put in. "Moving from check-in to the wireless network and then to the payment system, it could be a little glitchy, a little dodgy." He frowned, obviously trying to work through the glitches right then and there.

Guy could feel relief overtake the tension that had been building inside of him over the past weeks. "Glitchy and dodgy is okay," he said. "I'll gladly settle for glitchy and dodgy at this point. By next Friday, we need to write up three alternative versions of what Robert described to me."

He caught Hans's eye, interrupting the other man's mental planning. "Can Robert and I count on your cooperation for that? Within the next week, can you both help CellMobile get these three alternative approaches documented and evaluated?"

Hans and Vera promised they would. Then they resumed their technical conversation about wireless mesh networks. Guy thanked them and left the cafeteria with Robert.

"That was great, Guy," Robert said as they walked. "I think it might work."

"Maybe it will, maybe not," Guy responded. "I'm just glad to be back on track. We're alive again, at least through week six!"

Robert stopped walking and looked down at the linoleum floor. He seemed contrite. "I really appreciate what you told me earlier, about your friend Stanley," he said, looking back up at Guy. "I won't forget that. I'm so sorry you had to come all the way down from Philadelphia to tell it to me."

"No need to apologize," Guy told him. "If anything, I owe you and everyone else an apology. If I had taken Stanley's coaching to heart sooner, we all could have been spared a lot of trouble. So don't mention it."

And then Guy added, "The responsibility is all mine."

CHAPTER 18

X-Day

The world's first Shopper Xpress system was introduced on a sunny spring morning at the MegaMart store outside of Exton, Pennsylvania.

All the road signs leading to Exton had been changed to "Xton" for the day to mark the celebration. A crowd of thousands gathered in the MegaMart parking lot for the inaugural festivities, which would be followed by a huge 20-percent-off sale. A local rock band entertained the crowd, and images of the band were projected onto giant video screens at either end of the parking lot.

Since Exton is not far from Philadelphia, the entire crew from the original wave-and-pay working group had made it there for the celebration. Nigel had even flown in from London.

At 11:00 a.m. sharp, the video screens switched from the rock band to a view inside the store's sporting goods section. Petite Becky Campbell, a 12-year-old figure-skating champion from Exton, could be seen pulling on a pair of new rollerblades. The cameras followed her as she skated through the vacant aisles and approached the checkout area. Then came the moment everyone was waiting for: the first-ever Shopper Xpress transaction. Becky held up her cell phone, smiled, and glided past the checkout area on one foot, the other leg held out behind her in a graceful pose.

There were wild cheers from the crowd as an oversized register display lit up: "$34.95. 349 Megapoints. PAID."

Then more cheers erupted as the little girl emerged from the store into the sunlight waving her cell phone over her head.

The camera switched back to the store interior, where a young woman with a baby seated in her overflowing shopping cart approached the checkout area. A close-up shot showed that the baby was playing with a CellMobile cell phone. As the child and cart rolled past the checkout, a long list of items rapidly appeared on the register display with a total: "$69.86. 698 Megapoints. PAID." More cheers from the crowd.

Linda turned to Mike. "What's our total so far?" She was half-kidding, but Mike took the question seriously.

"Let's see," he murmured. His lips moved silently for a moment, then he began to think out loud. "We get a penny for every ten thousand Megapoints, which means we have banked, so far, a little over one-tenth of a cent."

"Pretty good!" Ted commented with a laugh. "We'll all be rolling in the dough in no time."

"Hey, it adds up!" insisted Nigel, amid more cheers from the crowd. Guy had no idea where he had found it, but somehow

Nigel had managed to acquire a bowtie adorned with tiny cell phones to mark the occasion.

At one corner of the parking lot, two steel ramps sat like bookends framing a dozen school buses parked side-by-side. The cameras inside the store showed stunt daredevil Bobby McKesson in a brilliant blue MegaMart jumpsuit and matching helmet, revving up a brand new 250cc motorbike.

"Are we supposed to believe this?" Nigel asked, looking worried. "He's about to risk his life on a motorbike freshly bought from MegaMart?"

"This is show business, Nigel," Ted replied, slapping Nigel's back. "This is America!"

Bobby McKesson revved the motorbike three times and then cruised down the wide store aisles toward the Shopper Xpress area. He held out his cell phone for the cameras. Then he slipped the phone inside his boot the instant before he passed through the Shopper Xpress zone. The register display lit up: "$3,249.75. 32,497 Megapoints. PAID."

An instant later, McKesson zipped out the front doors and picked up speed as he headed toward the eastern edge of the parking lot where the ramps and school buses were waiting. Then he was off, soaring 30 feet above the crowd, passing high over the school buses and landing safely on the other side.

"Guy!" Nigel called out above the wild cheers and applause. "In terms of difficulty, how would you say that stunt compares to running the working group?"

"There were many days when I would have gladly traded places with Bobby!" Guy joked. "At least, one way or another, it would have all been over quickly!"

"All right," said Mike. "That motorbike sale alone put us up over three cents earned today."

Guy felt a tap on his shoulder and turned around to see Robert Durham standing in front of him. The two shook hands and briefly hugged. Each was beaming at the sight of the other.

"I can hardly believe this is real," Robert told Guy. "None of this would have happened without you, Guy."

"Thanks, that's kind of you to say," Guy replied. Robert's comment reminded him of how close the project had come to collapse, and he quickly changed the subject. "How are you liking the new job?" he asked.

Robert had recently transferred from MegaMart to its Shopper Xpress subsidiary, which was jointly owned with CellMobile and Argosy.

"I'm really loving it," Robert shared. "Thanks for all your great advice. I'm on three different teams and working groups right now, and I'm not leading *any* of them!"

"Great news," said Guy with a smile. "But promise me one thing," he added, only half-kidding. "The next time you feel like complaining about your team leader, try to remember how much you disliked that job yourself."

Robert laughed with appreciation.

Guy turned to Ted and introduced him to Robert. The two exchanged polite pleasantries before Robert excused himself to rejoin his coworkers on the other side of the parking lot.

"So that's the infamous Robert," Ted said, nudging Guy with his elbow.

"He transferred from MegaMart last month to work for the subsidiary," Guy explained. "He's the big expert over there now, the only one who was with Shopper Xpress from the very beginning."

Ted shook his head in amazement. "You not only saved his bacon on that working group, but you helped him get a new job, too."

"A new *career*," Guy clarified. "He and I kept talking all the way through to the end of the working group. By the time we were done, he had decided that he wasn't cut out for the team leader role on these projects. It's no fun for him to lead, which means he isn't as effective in that position as someone else might be. This new job is a much better fit."

"I hope he knows how lucky he is," Ted said, looking at the MegaMart entrance, which was officially opening its doors to the crowd in the parking lot. "With all the shenanigans he put you through, you were a much better person than he ever deserved."

Guy shook his head. "I wouldn't talk about Robert that way," he replied. "What you call shenanigans was a normal response to lousy leadership, don't you think? I mean, for weeks I blamed him for avoiding confrontation when really I was the one who had that problem in spades."

The two men watched as consumers piled through the store's doors. After a few moments, Guy continued. "I nearly sank this project because I ducked my responsibility to get everyone to contribute until it was almost too late. I'll never forget that. No one can say I was a better person than Robert deserved because I know that he deserved even better."

Ted thought for a moment. "Well put," he said. He slapped Guy on the shoulder. "Thanks for the coaching! Now, what do you say we go check out this Shopper Xpress system in person?"

EPILOGUE

A Simple Fact of Life

When Guy pulled into his driveway later that evening, he saw Stanley outside watering the lawn. Guy locked the car and walked toward his neighbor, beaming from ear to ear.

"What are you so happy about?" Stanley asked him.

Stanley listened as Guy recounted his conversation with Ted at the MegaMart event. "A year ago I would have joined right in with Ted, bashing Robert for all the trouble he caused us," Guy explained. "We both would have had a good laugh. But now that feels wrong. Blaming Robert never did me any good. It only took my eye off the ball. It never helped me lead. So, when Ted started picking on Robert, I got really impatient with him. Robert's troubles were my responsibility from day one. End of story."

"That's accountability," Stanley said with a grin. "That's leadership. So how did Ted take it?"

"I think he was a little shocked for a second," Guy replied. "But he understood. He even thanked me. Ted Stone thanked *me* for coaching *him*."

Stanley laughed. "The student becomes the teacher," he observed. "That's excellent."

"I felt like I had to tell you about it right away," Guy said. "None of this could have happened without you."

"Now wait a minute," Stanley kidded. He cut the flow from the water hose and gave Guy a deadpan stare. "Don't blame me for MegaMart grabbing cash out of people's cell phones. That's your doing."

Guy laughed. "You know what I'm saying."

"Yes, and it's very kind of you," Stanley replied. "But keep the credit for yourself. Remember what it took for you to head down to MegaMart and have Robert's team get involved. You led without authority. You led in a matrix, with lots of moving parts beyond your control. That's the payoff from being truly accountable, and it's a hard thing to do. You know how hard it is because you resisted doing it until it was almost too late."

Guy shook his head, listening to the symphony of crickets around them. "I still can't believe how far I let things go," he admitted. "How close the project came to falling apart."

Stanley shifted his feet, squeezed the hose's handle, and started watering the flowers around his porch. "It's tempting to think of a person like Robert as a roadblock instead of a challenge," he said with a shrug. "A difficult team member can give a leader the perfect excuse to avoid conflict or disharmony. The blame is always plain to see on the other side of the table."

Guy nodded and watched the spray of water hit Stanley's flowers. "I told myself I was trying to work it out, trying to find a consensus," he recalled. "But all I did was delay a conflict that stared me right in the face from very early on."

"I'm going to drown these petunias if I don't stop watering them," Stanley observed. "If you have a few minutes, come sit with me on the sun porch. I've got a few questions for you."

The early evening light was fading. The birds in the large maple tree on Stanley's lawn started chattering as the two men settled into lounge chairs on the sun porch. "The first question I have for you is: What went well in your working group?" Stanley asked. "What did you do well from the start?"

"That's easy," Guy responded. "We had a very specific objective. We had SMART goals to get us there. I laid out my leadership philosophy and everyone worked together on the premise that while none of us had the answer, we all had pieces of the puzzle."

"Then what?" Stanley prompted. "What happened next?"

"The first problem was team members either not participating, or worse yet, not showing up," Guy said. "I asked Mike Andrews to leave the group and I replaced him with Freddie, but one key team member from MegaMart never did come to our meetings."

"What else?"

"Then MegaMart changed the objective from wave-and-pay to Shopper Xpress," Guy said. "CellMobile said it couldn't meet the Shopper Xpress technical specs, and Robert was too scared to even ask his team to consider CellMobile's concerns. It looked like we were deadlocked."

Guy chuckled. "Then I got really desperate and showed up at MegaMart uninvited. But it paid off. That one MegaMart team member who never came to meetings helped us arrive at a solution."

"So what will you do differently next time?" Stanley asked. He smiled, accentuating the crinkles at the corners of his eyes. "That's my last question."

"First, I have to address team member problems faster," Guy responded. "I need to get the right people fully on board as a top priority. I'll never forget how Freddie came up with that ingenious insight about check-in for Shopper Xpress. Freddie wouldn't even have been in the working group if I hadn't gone to Mike Andrews and asked him to start sending Freddie as a replacement."

"So that's one point of conflict you need to address right away," Stanley said. "Get the right people on the team and weed out the ones who don't belong."

"Also, at the first sign of conflict, I need to use more direct communication and coaching," Guy continued. "Robert was a source of trouble for the working group right from the start. I treated him with too much deference for far too long. That's not a mistake I'll make again. Instead, I'll assume a troubled team member needs my help, even if he or she won't ask for help and may be resistant to the coaching. The problem needs to be addressed."

Stanley nodded. "Leadership is all about how you handle conflict," he said. "And conflict is a simple fact of life. There's nothing inherently good or bad about it. There are only good ways and bad ways of handling it."

Guy stared at the maple tree for a long moment. "I'm not so sure, Stanley," he said.

"About what?"

"About conflict," Guy clarified. "I'm starting to think that for a leader, conflict is never bad. Conflict is an opportunity."

Stanley smiled and glanced sideways at Guy. "How do you figure that?"

"Look at MegaMart," Guy told him. "As soon as it looked like we had resolved all our differences and gotten wave-and-pay ready to go, MegaMart upped the ante. They went for Shopper Xpress, knowing it would cause conflicts in the working group, because conflict is where the opportunities are. There's an opportunity, maybe lots of opportunities, hidden inside every conflict that most people think is too difficult to deal with."

"That's an interesting point of view," Stanley commented.

"I think that may explain why MegaMart is the world's biggest retailer," Guy went on, lifting his hand to shade his eyes against the rays of the setting sun. "MegaMart wears down its partners and squeezes every penny out of suppliers as though it were always on the hunt for conflict. It executes through conflict because that's where the profits are. That's where the growth is. Once I look at conflict in these terms, I can't see the point in trying to avoid it or put it aside. Conflict is good, because every conflict presents an opportunity for a leader to make a difference."

Stanley looked at Guy. Was that newfound respect in his eyes?

"I never thought of it quite in that way," he shared with Guy. "But I do remember, on the *Constellation* refit, that the team was always better and stronger after we resolved a major point of conflict—at least, as long as I kept myself accountable and we didn't get into blame and finger-pointing. It's not always easy or pleasant to get through, but from the perspective of an accountable leader, I'd have to agree that conflict is good."

Now it was Guy's turn to do some kidding. "No need to thank me for the coaching, Stanley," he said. "If you ever need me, I'm right next door!"

ACADEMY LEADERSHIP SERVICES: DEVELOPING LEADERS YOUR PEOPLE WANT TO FOLLOW

In business, good management is about more than technical competency. To be truly successful, managers must also be leaders. That means having the ability to motivate and direct others toward achieving organizational goals. An effective leadership development program not only conveys those important lessons to participants but also shows them how to train their team members to do the same.

At Academy Leadership, we work with your organization to transform managers at all levels into effective leaders who can energize others to accomplish corporate objectives and create tangible business results.

Based on the leadership principles its founders learned at the Naval Academy and West Point—a passion to lead others, a persistence and drive to win, a focus on integrity, and the importance of clarifying each individual's contribution to the overall mission—Academy Leadership training, seminar, and keynote opportunities provide you and your staff with the essential skills you need to achieve business success.

Great leadership skills are at the pinnacle of what drives corporations to succeed. The best way to hardwire these leadership practices at your organization is through extensive and consistent training and leadership development. Read on to learn more about what Academy Leadership has to offer!

The Leadership Boot Camp

An intensive three-day leadership skills training program led by former corporate executives and service academy graduates, the Leadership Boot Camp is designed to transform your managers into leaders. This small-group seminar (limited to 15 people per session) shows your team how to improve business results by becoming better leaders. All who participate will come away more confident, more productive, more in-command, and better able to get things done through other people.

This is your team's chance to learn leadership *as it is taught at West Point and the Naval Academy* to the world's most successful military officers and future business leaders! The management and leadership skills taught at Leadership Boot Camp are based on military academy leadership principles and were developed and tested by an elite group of ex-military-officers-turned-entrepreneurs-and-CEOs. They have been battle-tested in the real world and are sure to generate real results for participants.

Send your organization's leaders to the Boot Camp and in return you'll receive men and women who are stronger leaders. They'll be transformed into effective managers who energize their teams, enable their people to see a clear relationship between their daily duties and organizational goals, communicate a consistent leadership philosophy throughout the organization, and instill smart work strategies in their team to achieve tangible results.

The Lead2Succeed Process™:
Creating Great Leaders and Sound Strategies
from the Top Down

Most managers are technically competent but often lack the ability to motivate and direct others to achieve organizational goals. The Lead2Succeed Process helps solve this problem by converting managers into leaders who:

- Seek responsibility.
- Hold themselves accountable for their own actions.
- Train their people as a team.
- Make sound and timely decisions.
- Communicate effectively.
- Plan for success.
- Create a positive, enthusiastic, and supportive environment in which their team members can be successful.

There are four distinct components—Leadership Assessment, Focus & Alignment Workshop, Application and Action Sessions, and Evaluation and Follow-up:

- **Leadership Assessment:** Identify what types of activities energize great leaders and what activities energize or frustrate team members.
- **Focus & Alignment Workshop:** Determine the *purpose, values, vision, mission,* and *goals* that will guide your company into the future and provide the common thread for developing leaders.
- **Application and Action Sessions:** Take part in the training and application of selected leadership topics. These sessions help participants create a common "leadership language" and enable those at each level to coach and mentor others as they undergo the program.
- **Evaluation and Follow-up:** Learn to use periodic measurements and reports to determine the progress being achieved in individual skill development and the overall program goals.

Our program is designed to achieve results based on your company's specified goals. Lead2Succeed helps your organization achieve company goals, inspires employees to take initiative in indentifying and completing tasks, fosters better communication from the top down to the bottom up, and motivates employees to give their best every day.

The Vision-Based Strategic Planning Process

Where will your organization be in 10, 20, or 30 years— on the *Fortune* 500 list or out of business? To know if you are succeeding as an organization, you have to know where you are headed. This six-day intensive, interactive workshop helps you and your team create your company's vision and the strategic plan that will help you achieve it.

In addition to the preparation of the vision and strategic plan, we also work with you and your team to develop a systems view of your organization. This enables you to consider options for improving your organizational and management structures and improve your overall business focus and performance. And since changing your corporate culture is often a critical part of the plan, we also incorporate processes for accomplishing that in the workshop, and develop strategies to continue it.

Our proven Vision-Based Planning Process creates for you and your team:

- A vision that is truly shared by all your leadership.
- Clearly defined top-level goals by which to achieve your vision.
- Clearly defined, quantitative objectives by which to achieve the goals.
- Strategies by which to achieve each objective, including strategies for cultural change.
- Action steps by which to accomplish each strategy.

- Implementation plan.
- Metrics—MOEs and MOPs.
- Assigned roles and responsibilities.
- Stakeholder strategies for gaining and keeping their support.
- A War Room report providing the logic trail.

At the end of the planning process, you'll have a vision that is shared by all your leadership, clearly defined top-level goals, strategies for achieving them, a strong, cohesive team, and much more.

Lessons from the Battlefields:
Academy Leadership Experiences Explore the Past to Help You Create a Better Future

The Gettysburg Leadership Experience. An excellent opportunity to gain a deeper understanding of leadership, teamwork, and communication, the Gettysburg Leadership Experience brings senior executive teams to the site of the greatest battle ever fought in North America. Through on-the-ground study of the leadership challenges faced by the commanders in this pivotal battle of the American Civil War, participants learn practical, usable lessons that will benefit their organizations today and beyond. Participants gain new insights and new ideas on:

- How leaders can make the right calls amid murky, ill-defined conditions, incomplete information, and high pressure.
- The intricacies of decision making and communication in very large organizations, and how culture affects what's possible.
- How successful leaders share their vision for success, reduce the possibility of misinterpretation, and get everyone pulling in the same direction.
- How leaders develop imagination and courage in themselves and others.
- Why character, a central element of leadership, is the key to building trust on teams.

Our experienced team of leader-facilitators uses stories of key leadership moments to bring critical lessons to life in vivid detail. These lessons, in turn, render valuable insights into how successful leaders operate today.

Modeled on the U.S. Army Staff Ride, a technique used to train officers in leadership and decision making, the experience lets participants see and feel, as no history book or mere lecture can, the challenges commanders faced during these three pivotal days in our nation's history. Instructors provide the historical background and facilitate in-depth discussion to reach a deep understanding of "leadership in action." Executives leave excited about their opportunities to be better leaders and armed with battle-tested tools they can use immediately.

The Normandy Leadership Experience. Learn how to lead at the site of one of the world's great military operations—the 1944 Allied liberation of France. During the four-day program, you'll see and feel the challenges that were faced by commanders in WWII's pivotal battle. Instructors illustrate "leadership in action" by facilitating in-depth discussion on topics such as the strong character of Dwight Eisenhower and how it kept the allies working together, how exceptional leadership led to the victory of Pegasus Bridge, and how leaders kept their soldiers moving forward in the face of adversity on Omaha Beach. During this one-of-a-kind learning opportunity, you'll gain new insights and new ideas on how to:

- Build flexible organizations that carry on in the midst of chaos and rapid change.
- Develop leaders who are creative thinkers.
- Communicate strategic intent so that everyone understands and takes responsibility for the mission.
- Earn the trust of subordinates.
- Build strong coalitions, across cultures and generations, for competition in the global marketplace.
- Prepare the next generation of leaders.

Best of all, you'll leave the experience armed with battle-tested tools you can use immediately.

The American Revolution Leadership Experience: Concord Bridge. In the Concord Leadership Experience, executives visit the Minute Man National Historic site near Concord, Massachusetts, flashpoint of the American Revolution, to learn timeless lessons on leadership that can invigorate today's businesses. During a visit to the site of this 1775 day-long battle, participants learn practical, usable lessons about team building, morale and courage, dealing with ambiguity, effective communication, and the execution of strategic intent. These powerful tools will help leaders to energize their organizations and get them moving towards their business goals.

As with our other on-the-ground leadership experiences, walking this historic ground creates a learning atmosphere that is almost impossible to create in a conference room, because the experience, like leadership, is emotional as well as intellectual. Executives gain new insights and new ideas on:

- How leaders help the organization combat fear and uncertainty.
- The intricacies of contingency planning and war-gaming.
- How an organization's culture can be predictive of performance.
- How leaders influence morale.
- How leaders organize effective teams.

Participants leave ready to meet the challenges of leading in today's complicated business world head on.

Out of the Trenches:
Inspirational Leadership Messages to Help Improve Your Organization

Are you looking for that perfect speaker or perfect subject for an annual company dinner, a professional association, or part of a larger event? The Academy Leadership staff has experience in speaking on a variety of leadership topics, such as leadership philosophy, productivity improvement, how to motivate people, how to manage conflict, how to develop future leaders, and more.

We can tailor a presentation to your audience and your specific needs. Whether you choose a keynote speech or one of our workshops, our programs will allow you to apply leadership principles to your organization's current situation. Your next company dinner could be the perfect opportunity to share valuable lessons in leadership with your staff.

Lead the Way Today!

If you would like to take part in one of Academy Leadership's results-driven workshops or training programs, or if you would like to book one of our speakers for your next company event, visit www.academyleadership.com or call us at 610-783-0630.

BOOKS FROM ACADEMY
LEADERSHIP PUBLISHING

The Accountability Compass: Moving from "The Blame Game" to Collaboration
(2012, ISBN: 978-0-9727323-9-0, $24.95)
by Dennis F. Haley

The Core Values Compass: Moving from Cynicism to a Core Values Culture
(2010, ISBN: 978-0-9727323-5-2, $24.95)
by Dennis F. Haley

The Corporate Compass: Providing Focus and Alignment to Stay the Course, 2nd Edition
(2009, ISBN: 978-0-9727323-6-9, $24.95)
by Ed Ruggero and Dennis F. Haley

My Father's Compass: Leadership Lessons for an Immigrant Son
(2006, ISBN: 978-0-9727323-4-5, $17.95)
by Perry J. Martini

The Leader's Compass: A Personal Leadership Philosophy Is Your Key to Success, 2nd Edition
(2005, ISBN: 978-0-9727323-1-4, $24.95)
by Ed Ruggero and Dennis F. Haley

Inspiring Leadership: Character and Ethics Matter
(2004, ISBN: 978-0-9727323-2-1, $24.95)
by R. Stewart Fisher and Perry J. Martini

Academy Leadership books are available at special quantity discounts to use as premiums and sales promotions, or for use in corporate training programs. For more information, please call Academy Leadership at 610-783-0630, visit www.academyleadership.com, or write to: 10120 Valley Forge Circle, King of Prussia, PA 19406.